I0013530

## Abstract

Since its inception in late 2008, Bitcoin has enjoyed a rapid growth, both in value and in the number of transactions. Its success is mostly due to innovative use of a peer-to-peer network to implement all aspects of a currency's lifecycle – from creation to its transfer between users. Bitcoin offers cash-like transactions that are near-instantaneous and non-refundable, while at the same time allowing truly global transactions, processed at the same speed as local ones. It offers a public transaction history, enabling trustless auditability, and it introduces many new and innovative use-cases such as smart property, micropayments, contracts, and escrow transactions for dispute mediation.

However, the same features that make Bitcoin attractive for its end-users are also its main limitations. Its decentralized nature limits the number of transactions and the speed at which transactions can be performed and confirmed. The problem with the slow confirmations is compounded with the semantics of the confirmations which are not final, requiring multiple confirmations and further delaying acceptance of a transaction.

In the first part of the thesis we analyze whether the current Bitcoin protocol scales and what the scalability limits are. We find that Bitcoin does not scale, because its synchronization mechanism, the blockchain, limits the maximum rate of transactions the network can process. In order to address the scalability problem we propose Duplex Micropayment Channels, which increase the rate at which Bitcoin transfers can be performed by several orders of magnitude, by moving the transfers off the blockchain and using the blockchain solely for dispute mediation.

Another form of scalability problem is the fact that more and more blockchain based applications are being created, each with their own small isolated blockchain, and vulnerable to attacks. We present PeerCensus, a subsystem that acts as a certification authority, manages peer identities in a peer-to-peer network and does not store application specific data in the blockchain. Using PeerCensus, any number of applications can share a single blockchain, decoupling confirmations from block generation rate and enhancing Bitcoin and similar systems with strong consistency.

Being a relatively new technology, Bitcoin has a number of new security challenges and innovative properties. We analyze these properties and challenges in the second part of the thesis. The first novel property is that the transaction history, in the form of the blockchain, is public and accessible by anyone. Making use of the open nature of the blockchain, we were able to dispell claims by MtGox, once the world's largest Bitcoin exchange, that a bug in the Bitcoin protocol was used in a large scale attack to defraud them. We then use the blockchain to build a prototype of an audit protocol that allows a fiduciary, such as a Bitcoin exchange, to demonstrate that its assets cover its liabilities, without resorting to trusted third parties.

Bitcoin also shifts the responsibility of managing and securing funds from a trusted third party to the end-user, which may not have the necessary tools to protect her funds. We show how a merchant may accept fast-payments, i.e., transactions without waiting for confirmations, with reasonable security against doublespending attacks by observing how transactions propagate in the network. Finally, we present a prototype of a secure device that stores private keys in tamper resitant storage and allows the user to independently verify a payment before authorizing it.

# Acknowledgements

My time as a PhD student in the Distributed Computing Group was exciting, instructive, and sometimes challenging and hectic, but I enjoyed every minute, thanks to the people that surrounded me. It is thanks to my colleagues, friends and family who made this thesis possible in the first place.

First and foremost I'd like to thank my supervisor Prof. Roger Wattenhofer for giving me the opportunity to make my, back then, hobby into my fulltime job, his constant support, and his open attitude to even the strangest ideas I could come up with. I'd like to thank Prof. Emin Gün Sirer for agreeing to be part of the PhD committee, taking the time to review the thesis and for his constructive, and enthusiastic, feedback.

I'd like to thank my office mate Philipp Brandes, who has suffered through so many Bitcoin discussions that he could give all my presentations by heart and for being a benevolent music dictator. I'd like to thank my colleagues at Disco (in alphabetical order): Georg Bachmeier for his team-building efforts, Pascal Bissig for being our fearless flyer and his pitch black humour, Sebastian Brandt for showing an archery enthusiast that quivers are cutting edge research, Benny Gächter for the countless hours of DevOps discussions, Barbara Keller for fighting for gender equality and leading by good example, Michael König for being the group's goto coder, be it games or work, Tobias Langner for being David fighting against Control Seminar mails and other Goliaths, Laura Peer for her simple approach to scheduling, Jochen Seidel, for the endless evenings and being the nicest and most honest byzantine I've ever met, David Stolz for showing me that in order to succeed you do not need to compromise on your ideals, Klaus Tycho-Förster for keeping morale high and feeding everybody with cakes, Jara Uitto for his unusual approach to clothes and for his convincing arguments to stick around, and Samuel Welten for showing that students are a useful resource. You are the reason I decided to pursue a PhD in the first place and had to suffer through my constant babbling about Bitcoin and the neverending thesis presentations about Bitcoin related projects.

Over the years I had the opportunity to supervise a number of student thesis, and I owe big thanks to the students: Tobias Bamert, Lennart Elsen, Jonas Nick, James Guthrie, Francisc Bungiu, Michael Voser, Cédric Waldburger, Fabian Schewetofski, Sandra Siby, Julian Fuchs, Pascal Widmer, Marc Müller, Stathakopoulou Chrysoula, Adrian van Schie, Matthias Lei, Renlord Yang and Filios Alexandros. I hope you enjoyed the projects as much as I did.

Last but not least I'd like to thank the most important people in my life: my family and my friends. Without their constant support and encouragement I would not have been able to embarque on this adventure, let alone succeed. In particular I'd like to thank my parents, Renate and Karsten Decker, for fostering my curiosity and raising me with an inquisitive mindset; and my brother, Martin Decker, both a friend and a fellow traveller on this voyage with whom I share so many good memories. A special thanks goes to my partner, Alice Schönenberger, for sharing all the moments of happyness with me and helping through the not so happy times. And finally I'd like to thank Dr. Hans-Ulrich Rentsch and Ursula Schönenberger for being the sweetest and kindest persons I have ever met and showing me what selflessness looks like. I have truly enjoyed every moment we shared.

# Contents

**10 Conclusion**

# 1

# Introduction

In late 2008 someone, using the pseudonym Satoshi Nakamoto, published a paper [68] on a cryptography mailing-list, introducing "a new electronic cash system that's fully peer-to-peer, with no trusted third party" [69]. The system is called Bitcoin and is based on the novel combination of cryptographic primitives, proof-of-work [11] and peer-to-peer technology. The core innovation of the paper is a distributed timestamping server that can be used to order arbitrary operations in a distributed system, and would later become known as the *blockchain*. Just a few weeks later the first implementation was published and the network started processing transactions, operated by a small number of tech enthusiasts. Although the identity of Satoshi Nakamoto remains elusive, today Bitcoin is all but unknown.

Bitcoin can be considered the first truly decentralized global currency. Over the last few years Bitcoin has grown from a small experiment by a handful of tech enthusiasts to a global payment system, with coins worth billions of dollars and an entire industry building on top of it. But what makes Bitcoin so successful? What are the core features that are attractive to its users?

Central to Bitcoin's success are its distributed nature and minimal requirement of trust among participants. It is an open, permissionless, system in which users are free to join, participate in the confirmation of transactions and be rewarded for their contribution. Bookkeeping is no longer performed by a trusted centralized entity, but by a collaborative distributed network of volunteers, in which individual actors may be malicious, but the majority can be trusted.

Transactions in Bitcoin are irreversible by design and near-instantaneous, independently of whether recipient and sender are in the same room or halfway around the world. These features make it a perfect fit for online payments, which so far were handled through intermediaries, with considerable time and cost overhead. In addition, it enables a number of novel applications, such as micropayments that were simply not feasible in traditional payment systems, due to prohibitively high fees.

Access to the Bitcoin network is easy, with a low entry barrier, allowing anybody with a connection to the Internet to participate and use it for payments. This opens up access to financial services to the millions of unbanked, people that so far were unable to have a bank account because it was not cost-efficient for banks to cater to them.

As with any new technology, Bitcoin also brings a set of new challenges to the table. We concentrate on two categories of challenges: the scalability and the security of Bitcoin. The first question is whether Bitcoin can process an increasing number of transactions as adoption grows. Sadly this is not the case. In order to independently verify the validity of transactions, each node in the network validates every transaction, stores it locally and tracks all coins in existence. As we show in Chapter 3 this does not scale well and the state of nodes may diverge for prolonged time.

One possible improvement, presented in Chapter 4, would be to use the blockchain exclusively to manage the identities of participating nodes, and process operations using a voting based agreement protocol. This would mean that operation processing is decoupled from the blockchain and a single blockchain could be used for any number of applications. The duplex micropayment channel protocol, presented in Chapter 5, on the other hand aims at processing most transfers off-blockchain, by routing payments over a network of long-lived channels, similar to how Internet traffic is routed nowadays. The Bitcoin blockchain is still used to setup and settle the micropayment channels. However, a single channel may process an arbitrary number of transfers before having to settle on the blockchain, alleviating the pressure on the latter.

In the second part we address Bitcoin's security related challenges. The open nature Bitcoin enables the creation of new security features that were not possible before. First we show in Chapter 6 how the public transaction history can be used to investigate the theft of 500 million USD from former Bitcoin exchange MtGox which was allegedly due to a bug in the Bitcoin protocol.

In Chapter 7 we show how the public transaction history can be used to audit businesses. Specifically we present a system that allows a business to prove to its customers that its liabilities are covered by its assets, without resorting to a trusted third party and without revealing any business critical information such as number of customers or list of assets.

While Bitcoin gives every participant the ability to manage its own funds, this liberty also comes with the burden to secure them and to protect against fraud. Chapter 8 shows how fast payments, i.e., payments in which the recipient does not wait for a confirmation, can be secured against double-spending attacks in which the same funds are spent in two different transactions. To address the issue of securing the funds we present a tamper resistent hardware wallet in Chapter 9 that can be used to independently verify transactions and sign them before broadcasting them to the network.

## 1.1   Collaborations and Contributions

Research is by definition a collaborative effort, either by basing the research on previous work or by working together on a result. This thesis is no different and it is based on a number of publications I worked on during my time as PhD student at the Distributed Computing Group at ETH Zurich under the supervision of Prof. Roger Wattenhofer. The results presented in this work were developed in collaboration with my colleagues in the group as well as with students working on projects I supervised. In the following I'd like to list the original publications and the collaborators that made them possible. Note that the authors are listed in alphabetical order and order does not represent merits in the works. Besides these collaborations all results in this thesis are also joint work with my supervisor Prof. Roger Wattenhofer.

**Chapter 4**   is based on the publication *Bitcoin Meets Strong Consistency*. Co-author was Jochen Seidel.

**Chapter 7**   is based on the semester thesis of James Guthrie which I supervised together with Jochen Seidel. It was published with the title *Making Bitcoin Exchanges Transparent*. Co-authors were James Guthrie and Jochen Seidel.

**Chapter 8**   is based on the group thesis of Tobias Bamert and Lennart Elsen which I supervised together with Samuel Welten, and with kind collaboration of Selecta AG. It was published with the title *Have a Snack, Pay with Bitcoins*. Co-authors were Tobias Bamert, Lennart Elsen and Samuel Welten.

**Chapter 9**   is based on the master thesis of Tobias Bamert which I supervised together with Samuel Welten. It was pub-

lished with the title *Bluewallet: The Secure Bitcoin Wallet.*
Co-authors were Tobias Bamert and Samuel Welten.

# Bitcoin

In this chapter we give a general overview about Bitcoin, adding the details that will be needed later. Depending on the context, the name Bitcoin may refer to any of the following three parts of the Bitcoin ecosystem:

- Bitcoin, the system: the abstract protocol introduced by Nakamoto in the original publication [68];

- bitcoins or BTC, the currency unit;

- bitcoind, the reference implementation. Written by Nakamoto as a proof-of-concept implementation, bitcoind still remains the most used Bitcoin client.

In this work we focus on the system and its protocol, in particular on how information is disseminated on the network. In Bitcoin two distinct types of information are disseminated:

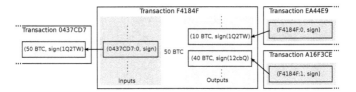

**Figure 2.1:** The first real transaction F4184F. It claims the 50 bitcoins output from transaction 0437CD7 and creates two outputs of 10 and 40 bitcoins respectively. Those outputs are then later claimed by transactions EA44E9 and A16F3CE.

*transactions* and *blocks*. Transactions are the primitives that allow the transfer of value, whereas blocks are used to synchronize state across all nodes in the network.

Unlike traditional currencies, like the US Dollar or the Euro, Bitcoin does not rely on a centralized authority to control the supply, distribution and verification of the validity of transactions. Bitcoin relies on a network of volunteers, to collectively implement a replicated *ledger*. The ledger tracks the balance of all accounts in the system. Each node keeps a complete replica of the ledger. It is crucial for the replicas of the ledger to be in a consistent state across all nodes at all times as the validity of transactions is verified against them.

## 2.1 Transactions

At an abstract level a transaction transfers bitcoins from one or more *source accounts* to one of more *destination accounts*. An account is in essence a public-/private-keypair.[1] An address derived from the public key is used to identify the account. To transfer bitcoins to an account a transaction is created with the address of the account as destination. To send bitcoins from an account, the transaction has to be signed with the private key

---

[1]Bitcoin currently uses ECDSA for the signatures.

associated with the sending account.[2]

Instead of aggregating the balance of each account, the ledger tracks *outputs* that transferred the bitcoins to the account. An output is a tuple of a numeric value in bitcoins and a condition to claim or spend that output. Hence, the balance of an account is the sum of the numeric values of all unspent outputs for that account.

Transactions are identified by the hash of their serialized representation (tx message). A transaction claims some outputs by providing a proof of ownership. The references to the claimed outputs along with the proofs of ownership form what is called an *input* to the transaction. The transaction may then specify one or more new outputs as destination.

Outputs are the fundamental unit of information that is tracked in the ledger and their status has to be consistent across all replicas. For a transaction to be valid the following criteria must be fulfilled by the outputs they claim and create:

- An output may be claimed at most once;

- New outputs are created solely as a result of a transaction;

- The sum of the values of the claimed outputs has to be greater or equal than the sum of the values of the newly allocated outputs.

As transactions are broadcast through the network the state of the ledger replicas changes. When a node receives a new transaction, it is verified and committed to the local replica. Over time the various replicas of the ledger at different nodes may become inconsistent:

- A node might receive a transaction that transfer coins from an account, but it did not yet receive the transaction that made those coins available to the account;

---

[2]The described method to send bitcoins to an account and claiming them by providing a signature is only one of the possible scenarios. We limit the description to this method here as it is the most commonly used method.

- Two or more transactions might attempt to transfer the
  same coins multiple time. This is called a *double spending
  attack*.

Double spending attacks have a direct impact on the consistency of the ledger replicas. During a double spend, whether
intentional or by mistake, two or more transactions attempt to
simultaneously claim the same output. The real world equivalent of double spending attacks would be a user that submits
multiple transactions to her bank, spending the available balance multiple times. While in this case the double spend attempt would be recognized by the bank and would not result
in a transfer, in Bitcoin this contradiction is harder to resolve.
A node receiving the first transaction will verify it and commit
it to its ledger replica. When the node later receives the other
transactions, the validation fails as the output has already been
spent. As there is no guarantee that all nodes receive the conflicting transactions in the same order, the nodes will disagree
about the validity of the conflicting transactions and any transaction that builds on top of them by claiming their outputs.

## 2.2   Blocks

In order for the ledger replicas to remain consistent a common
order over the transactions has to be agreed among the nodes.
Agreeing on a common order of transactions in a distributed
system is not trivial. Bitcoin solves this problem by tentatively
committing transactions and then synchronizing at regular intervals by broadcasting a *block* created by one of the nodes. A
block $b$ contains the set of transactions $\mathcal{T}_b$ that the node which
created the block has committed since the previous block. The
block is then distributed to all the nodes in the network and
each node receiving it will roll back the tentatively committed transactions since the last block and apply the transactions
from the current block.

At this point all the nodes have agreed on the validity of
all the transactions in the block. Transactions that were com-

mitted as part of the block are confirmed and do not have to be reapplied. The transactions that have been rolled back will then be validated again and reapplied on top of the new base state. Transactions that are now invalid because they conflict with transactions committed as part of the block are discarded.

The node that created the block effectively imposes its view of the changes since the previous block. However, the decisions of the block creator are limited. The node cannot forge any transactions as long as the underlying public-/private-key cryptosystem is secure. The block creator may only decide in which order transactions arrived and whether to include transactions in its block.

To determine which node may impose its view the nodes attempt to find a solution to a proof-of-work [34] with a given probability of success. The proof-of-work consists in finding a byte string, called *nonce*, that combined with the block header results in a hash $\mathcal{H}_b$ with a given number of leading zero-bits, or *target*. As cryptographic hashes are one-way functions, finding such a nonce can only be done by actually calculating the hash of the block for all possible nonces until a valid solution is found. It is therefore difficult to find an input that produces a solution, but straight forward to verify it. The nonce is part of the block so that nodes receiving it can verify that the creator solved the proof-of-work. The hash $\mathcal{H}_b$ is also used as the block's identity. The target is determined via consensus by all nodes in order to achieve an average of one result every 10 minutes in the entire network and is adjusted every 2016 blocks, which should occur once every 14 days in expectation.

Nodes attempting to find a solution to the proof-of-work are often called *miners*. To incentivize miners, the node finding a block receives a reward in the form of newly minted bitcoins, i.e., it may include a transaction that has no inputs but may specify outputs for a predetermined number of coins into the block. This reward transaction is only valid if it appears in the block and is the only exception to the rule that the sum of a transaction's outputs has to be smaller or equal to the sum of the transaction's inputs.

## 2.3   Blockchain

Up to this point, blocks do not provide any added synchronization on top of the individual transactions. This changes when the blocks are chained together, creating a chronological order over the blocks and therefore about the transactions contained within them.

The blocks are organized in a directed tree. Each block contains a reference to a previously found block. The block $b$ referenced by a block $b'$ is called its *parent*. The transitive closure of this relation gives its *ancestors*. The root block in the tree is the *genesis block*, which is hardcoded into the clients. This block is an ancestor of all blocks by definition.

The *blockchain* is defined as the longest path from any block to the genesis block. The distance between a block $b$ and the genesis is referred to as its *block height* $h_b$. The genesis block $g$ therefore has height $h_g = 0$. The block with maximal height, i.e., the block that is furthest away from the genesis block is referred to as *blockchain head*, with height $h_{\text{head}}$. We use the notation $\mathcal{B}_h$ to reference the set of blocks at height $h$.

Since to include a reference to the parent block, that parent block's identity (its hash) has to be known, the child block must have been found after the parent. The chaining is used to assign a chronological order to the transactions: transactions in lower height blocks have been verified before transactions in higher blocks.

As only blocks appearing in the blockchain will be rewarded with newly minted coins that are accepted by other users, miners will always attempt to find a block that builds on the current blockchain head. Building on an earlier block would require the resulting branch to become longer than the currently longest branch, i.e., the blockchain, to be rewarded.

## 2.4   Blockchain forks

From the definition of blockchain directly follows that there can be multiple heads at a time, i.e., when $|\mathcal{B}_h| > 1$ with $h = h_{\text{head}}$.

This situation is called a *blockchain fork*. During a blockchain fork the nodes in the network do not agree on which of the blocks in $\mathcal{B}_h$ is the current blockchain head.

Two blocks $b, b' \in \mathcal{B}_h$ are guaranteed to disagree about the current state of the ledger, because they both introduce a reward transaction. Hence, a blockchain fork implies that the system is no longer consistent.

When a node, whose blockchain head $b_h$ is at height $h$, receives a block $b_{h'}$ for height $h' > h$ it switches its blockchain head to this block. The new block $b_{h'}$ may either be on the same branch as $b_h$, i.e., $b_h$ is an ancestor of $b_{h'}$, or on another branch.

Should block $b_h$ be on the same branch as the newly found blockchain head $b_{h'}$ it will retrieve all intermediate blocks on the branch and apply their changes incrementally. On the other hand, should $b_{h'}$ be part of another branch, i.e., $b_h$ is not an ancestor of $b_{h'}$, then they share a common ancestor. Since $b_{h'}$ is on a longer chain than $b_h$ it becomes the new blockchain head, therefore the node has to revert all changes down to the common ancestor and apply the changes in the branch of $b_{h'}$.

A blockchain fork may be prolonged by the partitions of the network finding more blocks $\mathcal{B}_{h+1}, \mathcal{B}_{h+2}, \ldots$ building on their respective blockchain heads. Eventually one branch will be longer than the other branches, and the partitions that did not adopt this branch as theirs will switch over to this branch. At this point the blockchain fork is resolved and the ledger replicas are consistent up to the blockchain head. The blocks discarded by the blockchain resolution are referred to as *orphan blocks*.

Bitcoin never commits a transaction definitively. Every transaction can be invalidated if a longer chain that started below the block including the transaction is created. If a single entity could control a majority of the computational power on the network, and thus be able to find blocks faster than the rest of the network combined, it could revert any transaction. If an attacker attempts to revert a transaction that was included in block $b_h$ it would create a new transaction that conflicts with the original transaction and include it into a block $b_{h'}$ with $h' < h$. The attacker would then proceed to create blocks on top of $b_{h'}$ until this new chain overtakes the original blockchain and thus becomes the new blockchain.

One may argue that the existence of blockchain forks is the very reason that transactions are never definitively committed. The tight coupling between blocks and the validity of a transaction not only slows down the confirmation time of a transaction but also limits the confirmation to be a probabilistic statement about the validity.

# 3

# Information Propagation

The main problem Bitcoin sets out to solve is the distributed tracking and validation of transactions. For this, the network needs to reach a consensus about the balances of the accounts it tracks and which transactions are valid. Bitcoin achieves this goal with guarantees which are best described as eventual consistency: the various replicas may be temporarily inconsistent, but will eventually be synchronized to reflect a common transaction history.

As transactions are validated against the replica states, any inconsistency introduces uncertainty about the validity of a given transaction. Furthermore, an inconsistency may jeopardize the security of the consensus itself. This may facilitate an attacker that attempts to rewrite transaction history.

In this chapter we analyze Bitcoin from a networking perspective, i.e., how information is disseminated or propagated in the Bitcoin network, we identify key weaknesses as well as the resulting problems. In particular, we analyze the synchronization mechanism which fails to synchronize the information stored at the ledger with a non-negligible probability. This problem not only causes a prolonged inconsistency that goes unnoticed by a large number of nodes, but also weakens the system's defenses against attackers. We then propose some changes to the current protocol that, while not a solution to the intrinsic problems of the communication model used by Bitcoin, may mitigate them.

## 3.1   Information Propagation

The Bitcoin network is a network of homogeneous nodes. There are no coordinating roles and each node keeps a complete replica of all the information needed to verify the validity of incoming transactions. Each node verifies information it receives from other nodes independently and there is only minimal trust between the nodes.

### 3.1.1   Network topology

By construction the nodes in the network form a random graph. When a node joins the network it queries a number of DNS servers. These DNS servers are run by volunteers and return a random set of bootstrap nodes that are currently participating in the network. Once connected, the joining node learns about other nodes by asking their neighbors for known addresses and listening for spontaneous advertisements of new addresses. There is no explicit way to leave the network. The addresses of nodes that left the network linger for several hours before the other nodes purge them from their known addresses set. At the time of writing approximately 16000 unique addresses were advertised, of which approximately 3500 were reachable at a time.

Each node attempts to keep a minimum number of connections $p$ to other nodes open at all times. Should the number of open connections be below $p$ the node will randomly select an address from its set of known addresses and attempt to establish a connection. On the other side, incoming connection are not closed if they result in the number of open connections to be above the pool size $p$. The total number of open connections is therefore likely to be higher for nodes that also accept incoming connections.

We observed that a node running bitcoind which accepts incoming connections, has an average of 32 open connections. This greatly exceeds the default connection pool size of $p = 8$. On nodes that are not reachable, due to either being behind a network address translation or a firewall, the number of simultaneous open connections never exceeded $p$.

Partitions in the connection graph are not actively detected, and should they occur the partitions will continue operating independently. While this is certainly desirable from a liveness point of view, the state tracked in the partitions will diverge over time, creating two parallel and possibly incompatible transaction histories. It is therefore of paramount importance that network partitions are detected. Such detection could be done by tracking the observed aggregated computational power in the network. A rapid decrease in the block finding rate might indicate that a partition occurred.

### 3.1.2 Propagation Method

For the purpose of updating and synchronizing the ledger replicas only transaction (*tx*) and block (*block*) messages are relevant. These messages are far more common than any other message sent on the network and may grow to a considerable size. In order to avoid sending transaction and block messages to nodes that already received them from other nodes, they are not forwarded directly. Instead their availability is announced to the neighbors by sending them an *inv* message once the transaction or block has been completely verified. The inv message contains a set of transaction hashes and block hashes that have been received by the sender and are now available to be re-

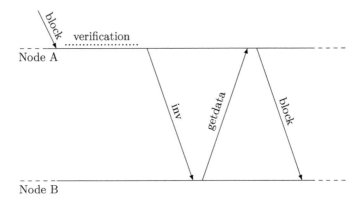

**Figure 3.1:** Messages exchanged in order to forward a block message a single hop from Node A to Node B.

quested. A node, receiving an inv message for a transaction or block that it does not yet have locally, will issue a *getdata* message to the sender of the inv message containing the hashes of the information it needs. The actual transfer of the block or transaction is done via individual block or tx messages. Figure 3.1 visualizes the protocol flow for a single hop in the broadcast. Node A receives a block, verifies it and announces it to its neighbors. Node B receives the inv message and, since it does not know about the block, it will issue a getdata message. Upon receiving the getdata message, Node A will deliver the block to Node B.

Each block or transaction is introduced to the network at one of the nodes, its *origin*, and is then propagated throughout the network using the above broadcast mechanism.

At each hop in the broadcast the message incurs in a *propagation delay*. The propagation delay is the combination of transmission time and the local verification of the block or transaction. The transmission time includes an announcement in the form of an inv message, a request from the receiving party and a delivery. While the inv and the getdata messages are relatively small in size (61B in most cases, as immediate broadcasts only contain a single block or transaction being announced), the block message may be very large — up to 500kB at the time of writing. Before the block is announced to the neighbors of a node, it is verified. The verification of a block includes the verification of each transaction in the block. Transaction verification in turn requires random access to data stored on discs.

Let $t_{i,j}$ be the time difference between the first announcement by the origin to the network and the time at which node $j$ receives the item $i$. If node $o$ is the origin of the data item $i$, i.e., either the finder of the block or the node that created the transaction, then $t_{i,o} = 0$.

The times $t_{i,j}$ at which nodes learn about the existence of a data item follow a double exponential behavior. Similar to randomized rumor spreading [48], the propagation of a data item can be divided into two phases: an initial exponential growth phase in which the most of the nodes receiving inv messages will request the corresponding data item as they do not have it yet, and an exponential shrinking phase in which most of the nodes receiving an announcement already have the corresponding data item.

To measure the propagation delay we implemented the bitcoin network protocol and connected to a large sample of nodes in the network. Our implementation behaves exactly like a normal node with one caveat: it does not relay inv messages, transactions or blocks. It tracks how transactions and blocks are propagated through the network by listening for the announcement of their availability in the form of inv messages. Once the measuring node receives an inv message containing the reference to a block we know that the node which sent the announcement has received and verified the block.

The measuring node collected timing information from block-chain height 180'000 for 10'000 blocks. The timing information contains the hash of the block, the announcing nodes IP and

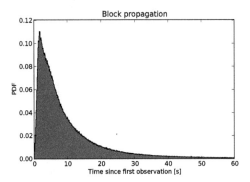

**Figure 3.2:** The normalized histogram of times since the first block announcement with fitted exponential curve.

a local timestamp when the announcement was received. An estimate for the $t_{i,j}$ is given by subtracting the timestamp of the first announcement of a block from all announcements for that data item.

Figure 3.2 shows the normalized histogram of $t_{b,j}$ for all blocks $b$ in the measured interval. The normalization allows us to use this as an approximation of the probability density function of the rate at which nodes learn about a block. Notice that we do not differentiate between the blocks' sizes and instead aggregate over all blocks. The median time until a node receives a block is 6.5 seconds whereas the mean is at 12.6 seconds. The long tail of the distribution means that even after 40 seconds there still are 5% of nodes that have not yet received the block.

### 3.1.3   Size Matters

There is a strong correlation between the size of a message and the propagation delay in the network. The *delay cost* is defined as the time delay each kilobyte causes to the dissemination of

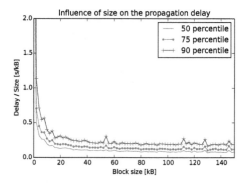

**Figure 3.3:** Delay costs for the 50, 75 and 90 percentile. The plot is focused on the lower y-range to show the constant behavior after 20kB.

a transaction or block. Notice that the cost is a combination of both verification and transmission time. Figure 3.3 plots the costs for the 50, 75 and 90 percentile for various sizes. For sizes larger than 20kB the cost can be said to be constant, whereas for small sizes there is a considerable overhead. The overhead for small sizes is caused by the roundtrip delay, i.e. the fact that even small messages are announced via an inv message and then retrieved via a getdata message. The roundtrip delay is dominant for transactions as 96% of all transactions are smaller than 1kB. For blocks, whose size is larger than 20kB, each kilobyte in size costs an additional 80ms delay until a majority knows about the block. It would therefore be sensible to forward transactions directly, and thus avoiding the overhead of the added roundtrip. However the same cannot be said for blocks where the overhead does not contribute as much to the overall time to disseminate.

### 3.1.4    Information Eclipsing

So far we have discussed how information is propagated in the case that the information is not contradicting. Another important part in the dissemination of information in the Bitcoin network is the visibility of information. When a node receives a new block or transaction, that it deems invalid, possibly because it contradicts information it received earlier, it will ignore it and not forward it.

Let us consider the case of a block being disseminated in the network and how it may lead to a blockchain fork that is only detected by a minority of the nodes.

Let $G = (V, E)$ be the network's underlying connection graph, $V$ being the set of all nodes and $E$ the set of connections between the nodes. Starting from a single partition $P_h \subset V$ containing all nodes whose blockchain head is at height $h$, i.e., they do not know any block for the next height $h + 1$. Finding a new block $b_{h+1}$ introduces a new partition $P_{h+1,b}$ which contains the nodes that believe this block to be the head, i.e., it is the first block for height $h + 1$ they received. If no other block is found, then nodes adjacent to the cut between $P_h$ and $P_{h+1,b}$ leave $P_h$ and join $P_{h+1,b}$ until $P_h$ is empty and the network as a whole proceeds with the new blockchain height $h + 1$.

On the other hand, should another block $b'_{h+1}$ for height $h + 1$ be found by a node in $P_h$, it again introduces a new partition $P_{h+1,b'}$. In this case nodes from $P_h$ will join $P_{h+1,b}$ and $P_{h+1,b'}$ concurrently until $P_h$ is empty, and all nodes are in one of the partitions with height $h + 1$.

Only nodes adjacent to the cut between $P_{h+1,b}$ and $P_{h+1,b'}$ will know both $b$ and $b'$ and therefore able to detect the resulting blockchain fork. Nodes that are in the partition $P_{h+1,b}$, and not adjacent to $P_{h+1,b'}$, will only know $b$ and be completely oblivious to the existence of a conflicting block. A partition $P_{h+1,b}$ could potentially contain only a single node, in the case that the node's neighbors already know a conflicting block and immediately stop the propagation of $b$.

The above also applies for transactions that are being propagated. If two transactions that attempt to spend the same output are propagated in the network only the first transaction a node receives will be deemed valid, the second transaction will be invalid according to that node's state and will therefore not be announced to its neighbors.

This behavior has the advantage that a malicious node may not flood the network by issuing hundreds of contradicting transactions with no additional cost, in the form of fees, to the malicious node. On the downside this very behavior makes double spend attacks that are invisible to the merchant [47] possible.

In the case of transactions, stopping the propagation is a reasonable trade off, that protects the network from transaction spam, at the expense of individual users. However, in the case of blocks, stopping the propagation is not reasonable. The blockchain forks, that are hidden from a majority of the nodes by doing so, are an important indicator of an ongoing unresolved inconsistency. As valid, but potentially conflicting blocks, cannot be created at an arbitrary rate like transactions, forwarding them would not create the possibility of an attack.

## 3.2 Blockchain Forks

In this section we focus on the block propagation and the blockchain forks that occur in the network. We show that blockchain forks are caused by the long propagation time by presenting a model that matches the observed blockchain fork rate.

### 3.2.1 Observing Blockchain forks

Some blockchain forks may be observed by participating in the network and receiving the two conflicting blocks. Observing all blockchain forks however is difficult. If a node detects that an incoming block conflicts with the block it believes to be the chain's head, then it will not propagate the block any further.

Recall that the partitions in a blockchain fork may have size 1. As a direct result, faithfully reporting all blockchain fork

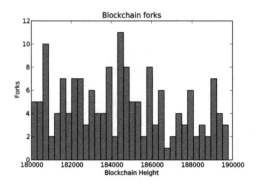

**Figure 3.4:** Histogram of blockchain forks for 10'000 blocks starting at height 180'000, observed while participating in the network.

would require being connected to every node in the network. Due to some nodes not being reachable, either because they are behind a firewall or network address translation, only an approximation of the actual number of blockchain forks can be given.

Using the implementation from Section 3.1 we collected the blocks that have been propagated in the network between height 180'000 and height 190'000. We are confident that due to our large sample, which includes all reachable nodes, nearly all the found blocks have been propagated to us, allowing us to identify close to all blockchain forks that occurred in the measurement interval.

Figure 3.4 shows the histogram of blockchain forks in the collected blocks. There were 169 blockchain forks in the observed 10'000 block interval, resulting in an observed blockchain fork rate $r = 1.69\%$.

### 3.2.2 Model

The proof-of-work causes valid blocks to be found independently at random. Since blocks are found independently at random by the participants in the network, a block might be found while a conflicting block is being propagated in the network. We claim that blockchain forks are caused by the block propagation delay in the network.

#### Probability of finding a block

The bitcoin protocol adjusts the difficulty of the proof-of-work required to find a block so that in expectation one block is found every 10 minutes.

If $X_b$ is the random variable of the time difference in seconds between a block being found and its predecessor being found, then the probability of a block being found by the network as a whole in any given second is

$$P_b = Pr[X_b < t + 1 | X_b \geq t] \approx 1/600 \qquad (3.1)$$

#### Part of the network that could find a conflicting block

A blockchain fork occurs if, during the propagation of a block $b$, a conflicting block $b'$ is found. Such a block $b'$ may only be found by the part of the network that does not yet know about $b$.

Let $t_j$ be the time in seconds at which node $j$ learns about the existence of $b$ since it has been found. Let the $I_j(t)$ be the indicator function whether node $j$ knows about $b$ at time $t$. Let $I(t)$ be the indicator function that counts the number of informed nodes, i.e., the nodes that have received and verified block $b$, at time $t$.

$$I_j(t) = \begin{cases} 0 & t_j > t \\ 1 & t_j \leq t \end{cases}$$

$$I(t) = \sum_{j \in V} I_j(t)$$

Then the ratio of informed nodes is

$$f(t) = \mathbb{E}[I(t)] \cdot n^{-1}$$

Notice that $f(t)$ is equivalent to the cumulative distribution function (CDF) of the rate at which peers are informed. We may therefore use the PDF of the rate at which peers are informed from Figure 3.2 as an estimate during the measurements.

Only the uninformed nodes may produce a conflicting block. Combining the probability of finding a block and the ratio of nodes that is uninformed we derive the probability of a blockchain fork. Let $F$ be a discrete random variable that counts the number of conflicting blocks being found while another block is being propagated, then the probability of a blockchain fork is:

$$Pr[F \geq 1] = 1 - (1 - P_b)^{\int_0^\infty (1 - f(t))dt} \qquad (3.2)$$

Notice that this last step requires the simplifying assumption that the probability of node finding a block is distributed uniformly at random among all nodes.

Hence, knowing the probability of the entire network to find a block $P_b$ and the distribution of how the nodes learn about the existence of the block allows to derive the probability of a blockchain fork. $P_b$ and the distribution of the $I_j$ depends on the computational power in the current network and the topology and size of the network.

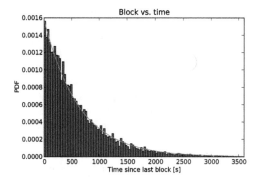

**Figure 3.5:** Shifted time difference distribution for blocks being found between height 180'000 and 190'000.

### 3.2.3 Measurements

To validate the model we compare the resulting probability of a blockchain fork with the observed rate of blockchain forks.

#### Probability of finding a block

Each block includes a timestamp of the time the block was found. As nodes do not synchronize clocks, but rather sample the current time of their neighbors, there is a non-trivial clock skew in the timestamps.

In some cases the clock skew is quite pronounced, producing even impossible constellations. For example block at height 209873 in the blockchain has a timestamp of 22:10:13 whereas the following block at height 209874 has a timestamp for 22:08:44. Since the latter includes the hash of the former, the blocks were found in the correct order. Thus the conflicting timestamps may only be caused by the non-synchronized clocks.

As alternative, because we are participating in the network and have a large sample of the nodes, we may also use the time we first saw the block being announced to the network as the time the block was found. While this does not suffer from clock skew, it may have a small delay between the block being found and the first announcement reaching the measurement node and we only have the timestamps the blocks that were found while actively measuring the network.

The proof-of-work is a Poisson process, therefore the time difference follows an exponential distribution. The convolution of the random clock skew and the time between blocks being found in the timestamp of the block causes a right shift of the maximum. This can be corrected by a left shift until the maximum is at $t = 0$. The announcement time observed while measuring does not suffer from the clock skew and directly produces the correct histogram.

$$g(t) = \lambda e^{-\lambda \cdot x}$$

By extracting the timestamps from blocks at height 180'000 through 190'000 we get the distribution shown in Figure 3.5. By fitting the observed distribution to the exponential distribution we find a value for $\lambda = 0.001578$ and therefore an expected time between two blocks of $1/\lambda = 633.68$ seconds. By fitting the probability density of the time between first announcements from the measurements we find a value $\lambda = 0.001576$ resulting in an expected time between two blocks of $1/\lambda = 634.17$. The two approximations of $\lambda$ are consistent, but both are slightly above the targeted value of 600 seconds. The difference is most likely due to a decrease in computational power in the network.[1]

**Block propagation in the network**

Due to the normalization the histogram in Figure 3.2 also represents the probability density function (PDF) of the random variables $t_{b,j}$ for all blocks $b$ in the measurement interval. Hence, the ratio of informed nodes $f(t)$ is the area under the histogram up to time $t$.

---

[1]See http://bitcoin.sipa.be/ for June 2012

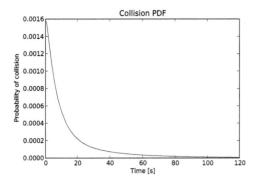

**Figure 3.6:** Probability density function of a conflicting block being found while another block is being broadcast.

Combining the above probability of finding a block and the function for the informed ratio results in the following probability for a blockchain fork:

$$
\begin{aligned}
Pr[F \geq 1] &= 1 - (1 - P_b)^{\int_0^\infty (1 - f(t))dt} \\
&= 1 - \left(1 - \frac{1}{633.68}\right)^{11.37} \\
&\approx 1.78\%.
\end{aligned}
\tag{3.3}
$$

According to our model the probability of a blockchain fork is therefore 1.78%. Comparing this result to the observed blockchain fork rate of 1.69% in Section 3.2.1 we observe that we overestimate the observed fork rate by only 5%. The slightly higher predicted probability is possibly due to the assumption that the computational power is uniformly distributed over all nodes in the network. However, the good quality of the fit suggests that the model is a good match for the reality.

Because the number of transactions and the size of the network is likely to grow as the adoption of Bitcoin as a payment method picks up the rate of blockchain forks is bound to increase. A larger network, with the random topology and the fixed connection pool size increases the diameter and the average distance between the nodes and the origin of a block. An increase in the number of transactions causes a growth in the block size which in turn increases the verification delay and the transmission delay at each hop in the propagation.

An alternative interpretation of the result in Eq. (3.3) is that each time a block is found, the equivalent of 11.37 seconds worth of computational power of the entire network is wasted. Work, i.e., attempts to find a proof-of-work solution, that goes into building alternative blockchain heads does not contribute to extend the blockchain, making it potentially easier for an attacker to overtake the current blockchain head with an alternative chain of its own. Nakamoto [68] already anticipated that an attacker with more than 50% of the computational power in the network would be able to find proof-of-work solutions faster than the rest of the network. The attacker would therefore be able to eventually replace the transaction history from an arbitrary point in time. While certainly sufficient, the condition is not strict, as our result shows. In reality the efficiency of the network as a whole, including a propagation delay, is not optimal. This inefficiency may give a prospective attacker that can reduce the delay a considerable advantage.

The effective computational power in the current network is

$$1 - \frac{11.37}{633.68} = 98.20\%.$$

Therefore, a 49.1%, share of the computational power in the network is enough for an attacker to eventually revert any transaction under current conditions. While even this is hard to achieve, increasing propagation delay may further weaken the network as a whole.

## 3.3 Speeding up the propagation

In the previous section we have shown that the way information is propagated in the network causes blockchain forks. In this section we explore what the limits of the existing protocol are and whether unilateral changes in the nodes behavior can change the blockchain fork rate. There are several ways to improve the propagation of information in the network:

- Minimize verification

- Pipelining block propagation

- Connectivity increase

Limiting the changes to the ones that can be enacted in an unilateral way allows us to assess their effectivity without major changes to the protocol, which would have to be vetted and accepted by the Bitcoin community.

### 3.3.1 Minimize verification

A major contributor to the propagation delay is the time it takes a node to verify a block before announcing it to the network. There is a strong correlation between the size of a block and the time to verify it. As each hop in the propagation has to verify the block before relaying it to its neighbors the delay is multiplied by the length of the propagation paths.

Currently there is a block size limit of 500kB per block enforced by bitcoind, but this is likely to be relaxed more and more as the average block size grows, so that it may include more transactions.

The first insight is that the verification can be divided into two phases:

- An initial difficulty check;

- A transaction validation.

The difficulty check consists of validating the proof-of-work by hashing the received block and comparing the hash against the current target difficulty. Additionally, it checks that the block is not a duplicate of a recent block and that it references a recent block as its predecessor to verify that the block is not a resubmission of an old block. The bulk of the validation is done in the transaction validation which checks the validity of each transaction in the block. The block can be relayed to the neighbors, as soon as the difficulty has been checked and before the transactions have to be verified.

Therefore the behavior of the node could be changed to send an inv message as soon as the difficulty check is done, instead of waiting for the considerably longer transaction validation to be finished.

Any change to the behavior of nodes in the network has to be vetted against the potential for being misused by an attacker to harm the network. In particular relaying information that has not been validated might allow an attacker to send arbitrary amounts of data that is then relayed, overwhelming some nodes in the network and resulting in a distributed denial of service attack.

This change does not increase the risk for a denial of service attack as producing an invalid block that passes the difficulty check is just as hard as producing a valid block with the same difficulty. On the downside this change is unlikely to have a large impact on the overall propagation delay if it is implemented only by a single node that is not well connected. It speeds up a single hop on the path from the origin to the nodes.

### 3.3.2   Pipelining block propagation

A further improvement can be achieved by immediately forwarding incoming *inv* messages to neighbors. The goal of this is to amortize the round-trip times between the node and its neighbors by preemptively announcing the availability of a block earlier than it actually is. The incoming *getdata* messages for

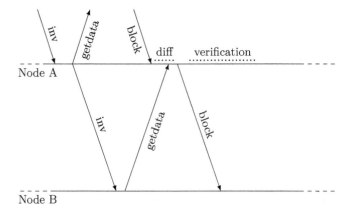

**Figure 3.7:** Message exchange after the behaviour described modifications. Compared to Figure 3.1 there is a notable difference. The *inv* message is forwarded immediately and the verification is split into two, speeding up the propagation.

the block are then queued until the block has been received and the above difficulty check has been performed, then the block is sent to the neighbors requesting it. Unlike the first change, this may cause some additional messages being sent as from the hash of the block no validation can be done. An attacker may announce an arbitrary number of blocks without being able to provide them when asked for it. Nodes receiving these spam announces will relay them to their neighbors. Should a node detect that one of its neighbors is announcing blocks that it cannot provide it can switch back to the original behavior of first verifying blocks before announcing them.

Even though nodes can be tricked into forwarding inv messages that it cannot provide the block for, the impact is likely to be small as the inv messages have a small constant size of 61B. Note that the same attack is already possible by creating an arbitrary amount of transactions and announcing them to the network. As the attacking node can provide the matching transaction, it will not be recognized as an attack.

Figure 3.1 and Figure 3.7 show the changes in the behavior. Node A is the node whose behavior has been altered. Notice the verification being divided into two phases (*diff* and *verification*) and the inv message being sent much earlier.

Again this speeds up a single hop and is unlikely to result in a large improvement if implemented only by single node in the network.

### 3.3.3   Connectivity increase

The most influential problem is the sheer distance between the origin of a transaction or a block and the nodes. To minimize the distance between any two nodes we attempted to connect to every node in the network creating a star sub-graph that is used as a central communication hub, speeding up the propagation of inv messages, blocks and transactions.

We instructed our implementation to keep a connection pool of 4000 connections open. This caused it to connect to every single advertised address, as fewer than 4000 nodes were reachable at any time.

The result is that the distance between any two nodes the hub connected to is close to 2.

### 3.3.4   Measurements

The above changes were implemented in our client and tested from blockchain height 200'000 to 210'000. During this time the client was connected to an average of 3048 nodes in the network and uploaded 20.5 million block messages. For each block the node received an average of 2048 requests.

Figure 3.8 shows the histogram of blockchain forks while participating in the network with the modified client. Comparing it to the unmodified case shown in Figure 3.4 a clear improvement is visible. The overall effect of the changes was

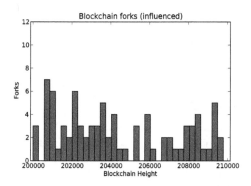

**Figure 3.8:** The histogram of detected blockchain forks while influencing the propagation in the network from blockchain height 200'000 to 210'000.

that the blockchain fork rate dropped from 1.69% to 0.78%, i.e., a 53.41% improvement over the unmodified case.

As mentioned before, the pipelining and the verification minimization only have a small effect, which is multiplied by the last change. The last change however has high bandwidth requirements as blocks caused bandwidth spikes up to around 100 MB/s and resulted in a total upload, during the measurements, of 2.31TB raw block data.

## 3.4 Related work

Although relatively young as a system, Bitcoin has sparked a lot of interest in many research areas. The topics that are being researched include the legal [1], the economic [16] and the technical aspects of Bitcoin.

The problem of double spending has been addressed in the original paper by Nakamoto, but only theoretically. Karame et al. [47] have an in depth analysis of the probability of a double spending attack to succeed in several scenarios. While they do mention the possibility of a double spend that cannot be detected simply by a longer detection period, we introduce the concept of information eclipsing, which causes this problem. Bamert et al. [14] propose some mitigations to the double-spending problem in fast payment scenarios.

Babaioff et al. [10] analyzed the incentives for nodes to forward information at all in the network and found that they are insufficient. A dominating strategy in the current system is for a miner to hold on to transactions that include fees, and claim them by eventually creating a block that includes the transaction.

Bitcoin mining requires specialized equipment and consumes large amounts of energy. Becker et al. [16] analyze the ecological impact of Bitcoin as a currency system compared to traditional currencies. Their conclusion is that while the fees to send a Bitcoin transaction are small, actually maintaining and securing the network against takeover is expensive. As we have shown the amount of computational power in the network is likely to be underestimated.

Another highly debated topic is the anonymity of Bitcoin transactions. The fact that all transactions are tracked in a replicated ledger and that the details of the transactions are therefore accessible by any participant in the network would suggest that privacy is not possible. However, Nakamoto claims that, since the identities of the owner of an account and the identity of the account are kept separate, the privacy can be said to be pseudonymous. Reid et al. [73] analyze this claim and point out that by colluding the information of multiple accounts that participated in a transaction details about the owner can in fact be recovered. Shamir et al [75] analyzed the transaction graph, deriving some global statistics, including an estimate that 78% of the issued bitcoins are not circulating, and an in depth analysis of a highly active region in the transaction graph. Elias [35] discussed some legal, and moral, aspects of the anonymity, or lack thereof, in Bitcoin.

The anonymity problem in Bitcoin was later addressed by ZeroCoin [58] which allows the implementation of a Zero-Knowledge based decentralized coin mixing service. Earlier Hanke et al. [39] presented a Pay-to-Contract Protocol that is built on top of Bitcoin and secures transactions between merchants and their clients. CommitCoin [28] is another system that builds on the blockchain to carbon date commitments.

## 3.5 Conclusion

In this chapter we analyzed how information in the Bitcoin network is disseminated in order to synchronize the ledger replicas. The reliance on blocks not only delays the clearing of transactions, but it also poses a threat to the network itself. Large blocks are propagated slowly in the network, giving an attacker an advantage.

We introduce a model that explains the existence of blockchain forks, and corroborate the model by matching it to our observations. As blockchain forks are symptomatic for an inconsistency in the ledger replicas, it is important that the nodes in the network are aware about them. However, due to information eclipsing, most nodes are unable to detect them.

Finally, we implemented and measured some changes to the Bitcoin protocol that reduce the risk of a blockchain fork. Our measurements show that a single node implementing these changes reduces the number of blockchain forks in the network by over 50%. The root cause of the problem however is intrinsic to the way information is propagated in the network. The changes may mitigate the problem in the short term, until a scalable long term solution is found.

# 4

# Bitcoin Meets Strong Consistency

Since its inception in 2008, the Bitcoin [68] cryptocurrency has been steadily growing in popularity. Today, Bitcoin has a market capitalization of about 5 billion USD. The Bitcoin network processes transactions worth approximately 60 million USD each day.

So, how usable are Bitcoins in everyday life? While one certainly can buy a coffee with Bitcoins, a Bitcoin transaction is shockingly insecure when compared to a cash (or credit card) transaction. Cash is exchanged on the spot with the coffee, and credit card companies are liable for fraud attempts. Bitcoins are different, as the Bitcoin system only guarantees eventual consistency. The barista will serve a coffee in exchange for a signed Bitcoin transaction by the customer. However, a signed

Bitcoin transaction is no guarantee that the Bitcoin transfer really takes place.

In order to get a better understanding, let us follow the path of our Bitcoin transaction. First, the barista will inject the signed transaction into the Bitcoin network, which is a random-topology peer-to-peer network. The correctness of the signature will be immediately verified by the peers that get the transaction. Next, the transaction will be flooded within the Bitcoin network, such that all peers in the Bitcoin network have seen the transaction. Eventually, the transaction will be included in a block, and finally the block will end up in the blockchain.

While the problem of fraudulent customers also exists with cash or credit cards, Bitcoins allow fraud on a whole different level. The main issue are so-called double-spend attacks [14,47]. Our coffee consumer may simply spend the same money multiple times. In addition to signing the transaction for our barista, the customer may concurrently sign another transactions spending the same Bitcoins but with the customer himself as beneficiary. While the barista is injecting her transaction into the Bitcoin network, the customer is injecting his transaction into the Bitcoin network as well, quickly and with as many peers as possible. Both the original and the double transactions will spread in the Bitcoin network, but the double-spend was injected at multiple vantage points, so it will spread more quickly. A professional fraudulent customer will manage that the double-spend transaction is orders of magnitude more present in the Bitcoin network than the original transaction. As such the double transaction will be much more likely to end up in a block, and ultimately in the blockchain.

The problem is that the barista cannot verify the whole process in real time. While injecting a transaction into the Bitcoin network, and the verification of the signature by the first peer is a matter of seconds, all the other steps in the process take time. Flooding transactions in a network already is an operation which may take minutes, and a block is only generated every 10 minutes [68]. However, with the current backlog,[1] it is unlikely that a transaction will be in the next block. Rather, a few blocks might be generated before our transaction (the original or the double) managed to be selected in a block, so for a low-value transaction like the payment of a coffee we can expect a delay of about 30 minutes. In addition there is the problem of blockchain forks [30], i.e., two conflicting blocks may generated at roughly the same time, and only subsequent blocks will determine which of the blocks is part of the blockchain and which one is discarded. Each subsequent block takes another 10 minutes, so in order to know that a transaction is confirmed, we may need to wait for several hours. The Bitcoin system is a prime example of eventual consistency: Eventually Bitcoin has a consistent view of the transactions, but one can never be sure, and it may always happen that a blockchain fork will destroy a substantial amount of transactions, sometimes even multiple hours later [4].

Because of this we argue that the current version of Bitcoin is fundamentally flawed when it comes to real time transactions, where goods or services are instantly exchanged for Bitcoins. How long should our barista wait until she is sure that the transaction will eventually be in the blockchain? Waiting for more confirmations does reduce the probability of the transaction being reverted, but how safe is safe enough? When should the seller release the goods or service to the buyer? Most vendors are probably unaware of this tradeoff between safety and time. In order to use Bitcoin for real time exchanges, we need to completely abandon the weak concept of eventual consistency and instead embrace strong consistency.

In this work we propose *PeerCensus*, a system upon which strongly consistent applications can be built. The basic idea is that Bitcoin's blockchain can be used to introduce and manage identities that participate in the system.

More precisely, PeerCensus uses the blockchain as a way to limit and certify new identities joining the system. This yields

---

[1] https://blockchain.info/unconfirmed-transactions

strong guarantees on the assignment of these identities to entities participating in it. We stress that PeerCensus is application agnostic, i.e., it does not manage any application specific information. A single PeerCensus instance may be shared by an arbitrary number of applications. In particular PeerCensus can be used to introduce strong consistency in Bitcoin. For easier readability, we call the strongly consistent Bitcoin that uses PeerCensus *Discoin*.

Discoin does not rely on its own blockchain. Instead, it can rely on a byzantine agreement protocol [25, 50, 51] to commit transactions to the transaction history, effectively decoupling block generation from transaction confirmation and thus enabling safe and fast transactions. Once a transaction is committed it cannot be reverted at any future time, a property we refer to as *forward security*. This is in contrast to Bitcoin, where confirmations are slow and can be reverted by a sufficiently strong attacker.

Our approach is also significant in light of the recent proliferation of alternative digital currencies, the so-called altcoins, all reliant on their own blockchain. The creation of altcoins has had the effect of splitting resources among many blockchains, resulting in many smaller and consequently more easily attackable blockchains. PeerCensus, with its shared instance, allows the computational resources to be concentrated to a single blockchain, strengthening it against attacks.

Moreover, PeerCensus enables experimental versions of Bitcoin to test protocol changes at a smaller scale before merging them with the main network. This is an alternative to the approach of [13], which instead suggests to allow transactions between otherwise separate blockchains.

The security guarantees of PeerCensus are extensively analyzed in Section 4.4, where we show that with high probability the system does not fail. Furthermore, we outline how the current Bitcoin system can be migrated to Discoin running on top of PeerCensus, gaining strong consistency and real-time payments as a result. Migrating resources and blocks from Bitcoin allows us to maintain the momentum and the public acceptance

Bitcoin has gathered over the years. Our proposed migration method results in an instance of PeerCensus that in expectation fails fewer than once every 7 million years.

## 4.1 Overview

Our main objective is to enable the creation of a cryptocurrency that provides forward security and supports fast confirmations. We accomplish this goal by leveraging techniques from Bitcoin as well as byzantine agreement protocols, resulting in strong consistency guarantees. Known agreement protocols are not applicable to a peer-to-peer environment in which Bitcoin operates, for three reasons: Openness, Sybil Attacks, and Churn.

- *Openness*: The set of peers eligible to participate in the protocol changes over time, but previous protocols rely on a fixed set of participants.

- *Sybil attacks*: Entities may participate in the protocol with an arbitrary number of identities, effectively disrupting voting based agreement protocols.

- *Churn*: Peers may join or leave the system at arbitrary times, therefore the quorum size required for agreement cannot be constant.

Voting based agreement protocols, like PBFT [25] and Zyzzyva [50], require knowledge of the membership: Before proceeding, the protocol must determine whether a sufficient number of participants voted. This requirement is in stark contrast to the openness of a peer-to-peer setting. Moreover, allowing unrestricted entry of new peers to the system creates the potential of Sybil attacks. In a Sybil attack, a single entity poses as an arbitrary number of peers (by generating fake identities) and joins the system as distinct participants in order to subvert the system. While the issue of churn has been addressed by previous agreement protocols (e.g., Secure Group Membership Protocol [74]), to the best of our knowledge Sybil attacks are left unaddressed by traditional agreement protocols.

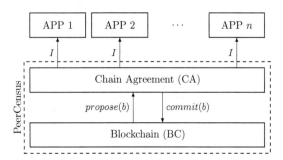

**Figure 4.1:** The layout of the components and information flows.

Bitcoin introduced a novel use of Proof-of-Work systems, namely a *blockchain* data structure, as a mechanism to deal with the problems caused by openness. But in Bitcoin states can temporarily diverge, since each peer applies incoming operations to its local state without reaching any kind of agreement beforehand. As a result, Bitcoin only guarantees eventual consistency, a property that is questionable for a protocol that is supposed to handle financial transactions.

In PeerCensus we combine those approaches to obtain the best of both worlds: Resilience to Sybil attacks and strong consistency. Correspondingly, PeerCensus consists of two core components: *Blockchain (BC)* and *Chain Agreement (CA)*.

The Blockchain's purpose is to mitigate Sybil attacks. This is achieved by regulating the rate at which identities gain privileges within the system, and by ensuring that those privileges are not obtained by a single entity. Peers are either *non-voting* or *voting* peers. In particular, new peers start as non-voting until promoted to *voting* by appending a block to the collaboratively maintained blockchain. The rate at which blocks can be found in the network can be regulated so that new identities are promoted at a fixed rate, currently every 10 minutes. Furthermore, the share of identities an entity may control converges to the share of computational resources it controls in the network.

The Chain Agreement on the other hand augments the system with strong consistency. By virtue of the voting rights issued from the Blockchain, a byzantine agreement protocol can be used. The CA's task is twofold. One task is to track the system membership, i.e., which identities are currently online and participating. This ensures that a voting based agreement protocol such as PBFT can function correctly.

The other task is to resolve conflicts in case of a blockchain fork, i.e., if multiple blocks are proposed for extending the blockchain, then only one of them will be committed. Using standard agreement protocol techniques we immediately obtain strong consistency. PeerCensus guarantees that with high probability, an entity can only subvert the agreement if it controls a sufficiently large share of all resources.

Applications built on top of PeerCensus may rely on the guarantees about the identity distribution and the membership. To demonstrate how simple it is to build strongly consistent applications on top of PeerCensus, we introduce a new cryptocurrency called Discoin. Because of the PeerCensus foundation, Discoin itself can rely on classical byzantine agreement protocols to atomically confirm transactions. Transactions are proposed to the primary in Discoin, which assigns sequence numbers to them and attempts to commit them to the transaction history. Since transactions are totally ordered, doublespends can be resolved locally, and upon committing all peers agree on a common transaction history.

Compared to the current Bitcoin system, Discoin and the underlying PeerCensus system have several advantages:

- A small blockchain since blocks only contain a single identity.

- Blockchain forks are resolved immediately when they occur.

- Confirmations are decoupled from blocks, enabling realtime confirmations.

- Since PeerCensus tracks the participating identities, Discoin can distribute rewards and transaction fees to all participants instead of just the block finder.

Ultimately, PeerCensus not only enables the creation of strongly consistent, but also simpler applications, by abstracting the dynamic membership.

## 4.2   System Model

The setting in which PeerCensus operates consists of the following three components: a) a *peer-to-peer* system, b) the notion of *controlling entities*, and c) the notion of computational *resources* at an entity's disposal. The role of the peer-to-peer system is to execute the PeerCensus protocol, whereas a controlling entity models an individual, possibly having control over several peers. A *Proof-of-Work* (PoW) mechanism (see Section 4.3.1) controls the entry rate of peers to the system to mitigate Sybil attacks. In particular, the amount of PoWs a controlling entity $e$ can generate, and thus the number of peers controlled by $e$ entering the system, is dictated by the amount of (computational) *resources* at $e$'s disposal.

**Peers and Identities**   We denote by $P$ the set of peers that may join the network. The *identities* (IDs) of peers are established using public-key cryptography as follows: When a peer $p \in P$ joins the network for the first time, $p$ generates a public-/private-keypair. The identity of peer $p$ is its public key (or a derivative thereof). We assume that there is no collision among the IDs chosen by the peers—in practice this is ensured by the assumption that obtaining the private key from the public key is computationally infeasible. We do not require that IDs are ordered, and the outcome of PeerCensus does not depend on the IDs chosen by the peers.

The system evolves in discrete unit time steps. At any given time, a peer $p \in P$ may either be online or offline, and we refer to the set of online peers at time $t$ by $P(t) \subseteq P$. Offline peers may *join* the network at arbitrary times, whereas online peers may *leave* the network by either halting (voluntarily) or crashing (involuntarily) at any time.

Peers communicate via message passing in a point-to-point network. This could either be viewed as having a completely connected communication graph, or by relaying messages among participants. We simply assume that between any two online peers there is a channel which eventually delivers all messages. The authenticity of every message is ensured by signing it with the sender's private key.

**Controlling Entities** The notion of collusion and shared control among multiple peers is formalized by introducing *controlling entities*. Each peer $p$ is assigned to exactly one entity $e$ which controls its behavior. The goal of $e$ is to steer $p$, hoping to maximize the entity's utility, i.e., entities are *selfish*.

**Resources** In order to model computational limitations of entities, we introduce the notion of a *computational unit-resource*, or *resource* for short. The set of unit-resources that will ever participate in the system is denoted by $R$, and $R(t) \subseteq R$ is the set of active resources at time $t$. Every resource in $R$ is associated to exactly one entity which owns it. All unit-resources are thought to possess the same computational power, and the more resources are active for an entity, the more computational tasks can be solved by that entity.

Similarly to peers, resources may exit the system voluntarily or because of failure. We assume that the failure and recovery probabilities of unit-resources are independent from their assignment to an entity.

## 4.3 Dynamic Membership Protocol

In this section we present the PeerCensus protocol which provides a trustless decentralized certification authority for identities. The PeerCensus protocol consists of three layers, namely

- the Blockchain (BC) layer,

- the Chain Agreement (CA) layer, and

- the Application (APP) layer.

We now turn to describing each layer separately, starting with the Blockchain, which is based on a Proof-of-Work mechanism.

### 4.3.1   Blockchain (BC)

**Proof-of-Work Mechanisms**   An integral tool used in the Blockchain protocol is a so called *Proof-of-Work* (PoW) mechanism. This concept was introduced by Dwork and Naor in [33]—we only give a brief overview in this subsection. The key insight behind PoW mechanisms is that that the resources needed to solve computational puzzles are not easily acquired and may not be scaled at will.

A function $\mathcal{F}(d, c, x) \rightarrow \{\text{true, false}\}$, where $d$ is a positive number, and $c$ and $x$ are bit-strings, is called a *PoW function* if it has following properties:

1. $\mathcal{F}(d, c, x)$ is fast to compute if $d, c$, and $x$ are given, and

2. for fixed parameters $d$ and $c$, finding $x$ so that $\mathcal{F}(d, c, x) =$ true using a unit-resource is distributed with $\exp(1/d)$, i.e., computationally difficult but feasible.

We refer to the parameters $d, c$, and $x$ as *difficulty, challenge,* and *nonce*, respectively. For example, $\mathcal{F}$ might return true if and only if the output of some cryptographic hash function to the concatenation $x|c$ starts with at least $d$ zeroes.

The PoW mechanism issues a difficulty and a challenge pair $(d, c)$. A nonce $x$ for which $\mathcal{F}(d, c, x) =$ true is called a *Proof-of-Work* for $(d, c)$. In our model, computational resources are required to find such an $x$. We assume that no entity has an unfair advantage in finding a PoW. Furthermore, we expect the PoW mechanism to automatically adjust the difficulty[2] between consecutive $(d, c)$ pairs so that the expected time for *any* resource to find a PoW for $(d, c)$ is some constant $\tau$.

**The Blockchain Protocol** The blockchain is a collaboratively maintained list whose function is to throttle joins of new identities to the CA protocol by employing a PoW mechanism. A single *block* in the blockchain has the form

$$b = \langle h, d, p, x \rangle,$$

where $h$ is a hash value, $d$ is a difficulty, $p \in P$ is a peer, and $x$ is a bit-string. We denote by $\mathcal{H}$ the hash function used to calculate $h$. A *blockchain* consists of a sequence $C = (b_1, \ldots, b_l)$ of blocks, and a *genesis block* $b_0$ that is fixed in advance. From here on, we assume the system implementation provides an agreed-upon genesis block.

For $i \geq 1$, block $b_i = \langle h, d, p, x \rangle$ is said to be *legal* if

$$
\begin{aligned}
h &= \mathcal{H}(b_{i-1}), \text{ and} \\
\mathcal{F}(d, \langle h, p \rangle, x) &= \text{true},
\end{aligned}
$$

that is, if the hash in $b_i$ is obtained from $b_{i-1}$, and $b_i$ is a Proof-of-Work. For a legal block $b_i$, the block $b_{i-1}$ is called the *parent* of $b_i$, and $b_i$ is a *child* of $b_{i-1}$. A blockchain is *legal* if every non-genesis block is legal.

Since the blockhain is based on a PoW mechanism it is ensured that new blocks cannot be appended to $C$ at will. Attempting to find a legal block that extends the current blockchain is called *mining*. We encapsulate this process in the procedure $\mathtt{mine}(b)$, which for peer $p$ attempts to find a block with parent $b$ that includes $p$'s identity.

Note that legal blocks together with $b_0$ form a tree rooted at $b_0$ due to the parent/child relation, and a legal blockchain corresponds to a path in the tree starting at the root. In order to provide forward security, it is necessary that once the peers agree on a blockchain $C$, they will never accept a blockchain

---

[2]The PoW mechanism used by Bitcoin accomplishes this (cf. [68]).

---

**Protocol:** Blockchain, from the perspective of peer $p$
**Initialization:**

> $C \leftarrow$ the current Blockchain, obtained from CA
> trigger Start event

**On Event** *Start*:
> $b \leftarrow$ the newest block in $C$
> `mine`($b$)

**On Event** `mine` *(b) returns block $b^*$*:
> `propose_block`($b^*$) using CA

**On Event** *CA commits a block a*:
> stop mining
> $C \leftarrow$ the new blockchain from CA
> if $a \neq b^*$ **then**
>> trigger Start event

---

**Figure 4.2:** The Blockchain Protocol.

that does not have $C$ as a prefix. To tackle this issue, whenever the blockchain is extended the CA protocol is used to ensure that all peers agree on the same extended blockchain. In particular, the BC protocol relies on the `propose_block` operation provided by the Chain Agreement.

If the Chain Agreement protocol accepts the block proposed by peer $p$, then the identity of $p$ becomes voting. In that case the resources allocated to $p$'s mining process by the controlling entity of $p$ may be assigned to a new identity. If on the other hand a block containing a different peer is accepted, then $p$ continues mining and proposes the next block it finds. Refer to Fig. 4.2 for a pseudo-code description of the BC protocol.

### 4.3.2   Chain Agreement (CA)

While the blockchain introduces new identities into the system, the Chain Agreement tracks the membership of currently participating identities in the system. For our CA protocol we adapt SGMP [74] and the PBFT [25] agreement protocols. In particular, the goal is to keep track of some *shared state* that can be modified by certain predetermined *operations*. In our case, the shared state encompasses an *operation log O*, a set of *online voters I*, and the blockchain *C*.

As in SGMP and PBFT, the life cycle of an operation *op* begins with *op*'s *proposal*. The proposal is sent to the *primary*, i.e., to a specific peer determined by an agreed-upon scheme. Given that *op* is valid and the peers decide to commit it, *op* is applied to the shared state. Both agreement protocols rely on the notion of totally ordered *logical time stamps*, and in each such time step exactly one operation is committed. A *logical time stamp* is a triple $(\ell, v, s)$, where $\ell$ is the current length of $C$ (i.e., the blockchain contained in the shared state), and $v$ and $s$ are positive integers referred to as the *view primary number* and *sequence number*, respectively. Logical time stamps are ordered in lexicographic order.

To determine the primary we introduce the notion of a peer's rank. For a fixed blockchain $C = (b_1, \ldots, b_\ell)$ and a voting peer $p$ let $i$ denote the index of the block in which $p$ appears. The *rank of p*, denoted by $\text{rank}(C, p)$, is $\ell - i$, i.e., peers are ranked by how recently the right to vote was obtained. Note that the rank is well defined since a peer can acquire the right to vote only once.

Consider a time stamp $(\ell, v, s)$ and the associated blockchain $C$ of length $\ell$. The peer $p$ with $\text{rank}(C, p) = v \pmod{\ell}$ is chosen as the primary, i.e., the peer who accepts operation proposals for the next time step. We use the failover mechanism of PBFT to ensure that $v$ is increased without the help of a primary in case the current primary fails.

Using the logical time stamps and the rank as fixed above, the underlying SGMP/PBFT agreement protocols can be used to implement Chain Agreement. Note however that due to churn, just like SGMP, CA cannot support a snapshot mechanism. This is in contrast to PBFT where the set of participating peers is fixed in advance and snapshots are supported.

**Operations**    The Chain Agreement uses a standard byzantine
agreement technique, in which each operation has to go through
the stages propose, pre-prepare, prepare, and commit before it
is applied. More specifically, operations are initially proposed
to the current primary $q$. The task of $q$ is to assign consecutive
time stamps to proposed operations. For each proposal, $q$ then
sends out pre-prepare messages, receives prepare messages, and
commits the operation once $q$ received a sufficient amount of
prepare messages from peers in $I$. Recall that in each step,
authenticity of messages is guaranteed due to signatures offered
by the public key cryptography system.

What is left in the Chain Agreement specification are the
operations mutating the shared state. The Chain Agreement
protocol relies on the following three operations:

- $\texttt{block}(b)$ is used to append a new block $b$ to the Blockchain, thus promoting the peer contained in $b$ to be promoted to voting.

- $\texttt{join}(p)$ is used by a previously offline voting peer $p$ to
  re-join the set $I$ of online voters.

- $\texttt{leave}(p)$ is used to remove offline peers from $I$.

We need to explicate two aspects of each operation, namely
how the operation *validated*, and how *committing* it affects the
shared state. Validation occurs at the primary when an operation is proposed, and at other nodes upon receiving a pre-
prepare message for that operation. This is to ensure that a
faulty/malicious user cannot modify the shared state in an un-
desired manner. Whenever an operation is committed, peers
append the operation together with its assigned time stamp
and collected commit signatures to the operation log and update their new time stamp accordingly. Furthermore, committing an operation may modify the shared state according to the
operation's purpose. We now describe both aspects for each
operation separately and refer to Fig. 4.3 for a pseudo-code
description.

---

**Specification:** Operations for Chain Agreement

**Shared State:**

| $O$ | ▷ *The operation log* |
| $I$ | ▷ *The set of online voters* |
| $C$ | ▷ *The blockchain* |
| $t = (\ell, v, s)$ | ▷ *The logical time stamp* |

**Validate** block($b$)**:**
> $b' \leftarrow$ the newest block in $C$
> **if** *b is a child of $b'$ and b is legal* **then**
> | **return** valid
> **else**
> └ **return** invalid

**On Commit** block($b$)**:**
> Append block($b$) to $O$
> Append $b$ to $C$
> $\langle h, d, p, x \rangle \leftarrow b$
> $I \leftarrow I \cup \{p\}$         ▷ *Promote p to voting*
> $\ell \leftarrow$ the length of $C$     ▷ *Update logical time stamp*
> $v \leftarrow 0$
> $s \leftarrow 0$

**Validate** join($p$)**:**
> Send a ping message to $p$
> $V \leftarrow$ the set of peers appearing in the blocks of $C$
> **if** $p \in V$, $p \notin I$, *and p replies to the ping* **then**
> | **return** valid
> **else**
> └ **return** invalid

**On Commit** join($p$)**:**
> Append join($p$) to $O$
> $I \leftarrow I \cup \{p\}$

**Validate** leave($p$)**:**
> Send a ping message to $p$
> **if** $p \in I$ *and p does not reply* **then**
> | **return** valid
> **else**
> └ **return** invalid

**On Commit** leave($p$)**:**
> Append leave($p$) to $O$
> $I \leftarrow I \setminus \{p\}$

---

**Figure 4.3:** Operations of the Chain Agreement Protocol

Recall that proposals for a block $b$ are sent to the Chain Agreement only from the Blockchain layer. To validate a $\mathtt{block}(b)$ operation, all peers check that $b$ is indeed valid and extends the current blockchain $C$. To commit this operation $b$ is appended to $C$, and the time stamp is set to $(\ell, 0, 0)$, where $\ell$ is the new blockchain length. This results in the block finder becoming the new primary, with the previous primary as backup.

A join operation consists of the joining peer $p$. To validate a join, peers check whether $p$ is indeed reachable over the network. In that case, the operation will be committed and $p$ is included in the set $I$.

Peers rely on a failure detector to detect when identities left the system, e.g., by sending *ping* messages in regular intervals. Should one peer detect a failure of another peer $p$, a leave operation on behalf of $p$ will be emitted. A $\mathtt{leave}(p)$ operation is validated by checking whether $p$ indeed failed, to keep malicious peers from removing online peers. When the operation turns out to be valid, it is committed by removing $p$ from $I$.

### 4.3.3   Application

The application layer makes use of the membership information from the CA in order to implement the application logic. The CA provides a ranking among identities, the current membership as well as its timestamp, which enables the application to use the full capabilities of PBFT. This includes the use of snapshots of the application state.

The application has some shared state and deterministic operations that modify the state. Operations are totally ordered by assigning a timestamp $(t, o)$ to them, where $t$ is the membership timestamp from the CA and $o$ is an *operation sequence number* assigned by the current primary.

The application logic and state is encapsulated in the application layer and does not influence the decisions in the CA. A single instance of the CA and the BC can therefore be shared among any number of applications.

Applications may export functionality to clients that are not participating in the application agreement. Clients synchronize with the CA in order to get the membership information. The synchronization consists of downloading the CA operation log and incrementally applying it to the membership. The clients then submit operations to the application, which in turn processes them. Using the membership information, the clients then verify the confirmation that the operation was processed correctly.

## 4.4 Safety & Liveness

We would like to lift the safety and liveness guarantees provided by PBFT [24] and apply them to our Chain Agreement. An agreement protocol provides *safety* if operations on the shared state are committed atomically, i.e., as if they were applied on a single sequential machine; An agreement protocol provides *liveness* if all proposed valid operations are eventually committed. The premise under which PBFT provides both is that less than one third of the participants are not faulty.

In our setting participants in the *protocol* are modeled as peers, whereas participants in the *system*, i.e., a individuals with an agenda to subvert the protocol, are modeled as *entities*. In order to lift the guarantees from PBFT to Chain Agreement, we need to ensure that at any time $t$, less than one third of the online voters (the set $I$ in the CA) are controlled by a single entity. Since SGMP ensures that $I$ tracks the voters in $P(t)$ (with some delay depending on the message delays and failure detector speeds, cf. [74]), it is sufficient to investigate how $P(t)$, and in particular the voters therein, evolves over time.

To state this formally, let $A$ be a malicious entity referred to as *attacker*. To simplify the analysis, we denote by $D$ a meta-entity that encompasses all entities that are not $A$. For some fixed point in time, let $I$ be the set of online voters. We denote by $I_A$, and $I_D$ the corresponding partition of $I$ into online peers controlled $A$, and $D$, respectively. We can apply the classic positive results for byzantine agreement due to Lamport [71] if it holds that $|I_A|/|I| < 1/3$. This is equivalent to ensuring that

$$\phi_I := \frac{|I_A|}{|I_D|} < 1/2\,.$$

Therefore, as long as the inequality remains satisfied we say that PeerCensus is in a *secure state*. On the other hand, Lamport's work also established that no guarantees can be made should the inequality be exceeded. Correspondingly, when the inequality is violated we say that PeerCensus is in an *insecure state*.

What are the consequences of being in an insecure state? First observe that $A$ can cement its control by not committing block or join operations, thus hindering peers controlled by other entities from being included the online voter set. The effect for the application layer is that new operations are only applied at $A$'s will. Note however, that past committed operations cannot be modified or undone by any attack on the protocol, i.e., strong consistency up to the time when $A$ took control is still guaranteed.

Our analysis relies on the system being in its *steady state*, i.e., that the number of online peers and resources is governed by the respective expected value. This is the case if PeerCensus was active for a sufficiently long time. Later in Section 4.4.3 we show that this assumption is justified due to a bootstrapping method. Before describing the procedure in detail, we now turn to establishing our following main theorem.

**Theorem 1.** *Let $\phi_R$ denote the fraction of resources associated with $A$ over resources not associated with $A$, and let $0 < \epsilon < 1/2$ be a constant. If PeerCensus reaches a steady state and $\phi_R < 1/2 - \epsilon$, then PeerCensus is in a secure state with high probability.*

To prove Theorem 1 we separately consider the three factors that influence the cardinalities of $I_A$ and $I_D$, namely membership churn, resource churn and miner's luck.

- *Resource churn*: Resources fail and recover, thus limiting or enhancing the attacker's capability to introduce new peers to the voter set.

- *Membership churn*: Voting peers fail and recover, directly affecting $I_A$ as well as $I_D$.

- *Miner's luck*: A stochastic block mining process determines who gets to introduce a new peer to the voter set. With non-zero probability, an attacker's resources may mine more blocks than expected, thus increasing $P_A$ disproportionately.

### 4.4.1 Preliminaries

In the steady state, resource churn is characterized by a parameter $\rho$ in the following way. The state of an individual resource is modeled as a two-state Markov-Chain with the transition matrix

$$\begin{pmatrix} 1-p & p \\ q & 1-q \end{pmatrix},$$

where $p$ and $q$ denote the probability of a resource to fail or recover, respectively. The two states indicate whether the resource is currently active, or inactive. For a single resource, the stationary distribution is $(\rho, 1-\rho)$, where $\rho = q/(p+q)$. We conclude that in the steady state the expected number of online resources is $\rho|R|$, since resources fail or recover independently from one another.

**Lemma 1.** *Let $\phi_R$ be the random variable representing the ratio of online resources for A to online resources for D. In the steady state and for $\alpha \in (0, 1/2)$ it holds that*

$$\Pr\left[\phi_R \geq \left(1 + \frac{2\alpha}{1-\alpha}\right)r\right] < \left(\frac{\exp(\alpha)}{(1+\alpha)^{1+\alpha}}\right)^{\rho n r/(1+r)}$$
$$+ \left(\frac{\exp(-\alpha)}{(1-\alpha)^{1-\alpha}}\right)^{\rho n/(1+r)},$$

*where $n$ is the cardinality of $R$, and $r$ is the ratio of $A$'s resources to $D$'s resources in $R$.*

*Proof.* Denote by $R_A \dot{\cup} R_D = R$ the partition of $R$ into resources belonging to the attacker $A$ and defender $D$. For $i \in R_A$, let $X_i$ be the 0/1 random variable indicating whether resource $i$ is online. Correspondingly for $j \in R_D$, let $Y_j$ be the 0/1 random variable indicating whether resource $j$ is online. Let $X$ and $Y$ be the corresponding random variables denoting the sum of $X_i$ and $Y_j$. Note that in the stationary distribution, the expected value of $X$ and $Y$ are $\rho|R_A|$ and $\rho|R_D|$, respectively.

With these definitions $\phi_R = X/Y$. Since $X$ and $Y$ are independent it holds that $E[\phi_R] = E[X]/E[Y] = r$. Our goal is to bound the probability that $\phi_R$ deviates from its expected value by bounding the probability of $X$ and $Y$ deviating from their expected values. Applying the Chernoff bound (see, e.g., [62]) to $X$ and $Y$ yields that

$$\Pr[X > (1 + \beta)\rho|R_A|] < \left( \frac{\exp(\beta)}{(1+\beta)^{1+\beta}} \right)^{\rho|R_A|} \text{ , and}$$

$$\Pr[Y < (1 - \gamma)\rho|R_D|] < \left( \frac{\exp(-\gamma)}{(1-\gamma)^{1-\gamma}} \right)^{\rho|R_D|}$$

for any $\beta > 0$ and $0 < \gamma < 1$. Let $\mathbf{X}(\beta)$ and $\mathbf{Y}(\gamma)$ denote the two events from above, i.e., that $X$ resp. $Y$ deviates from the corresponding expected value by $(1+\beta)$ and $(1-\gamma)$.

Let $\mathbf{Z}$ denote the event that $\phi_R > (1 + 2\alpha)r$, i.e., the event from the statement, and consider positive values $\beta$ and $\gamma$ such that $\beta + \gamma = 2\alpha$. If neither $\mathbf{X}(\beta)$ nor $\mathbf{Y}(\gamma)$ occurs, then also $\mathbf{Z}$ does not occur. By applying the union bound we obtain

$$\Pr[\mathbf{Z}] \leq \Pr[\mathbf{X}(\beta) \vee \mathbf{Y}(\gamma)] \leq \Pr[\mathbf{X}(\beta)] + \Pr[\mathbf{Y}(\gamma)] \,.$$

We bound the above by applying the previously obtained Chernoff bounds for $\mathbf{X}(\beta)$ and $\mathbf{Y}(\gamma)$. Doing so yields

$$\Pr[\mathbf{Z}] < \left( \frac{\exp(\beta)}{(1+\beta)^{1+\beta}} \right)^{\rho|R_A|} + \left( \frac{\exp(-\gamma)}{(1-\gamma)^{1-\gamma}} \right)^{\rho|R_D|} \,.$$

This resulting sum is minimized if $\beta = \gamma$, i.e., $\alpha = 2\beta/(1 - \beta)$. By observing that $|R_A| = nr/(1 + r)$ and $|R_D| = n/(1 + r)$ the proof is completed. $\qquad\square$

Lemma 1 bounds the impact of resource churn. Our next goal is to do the same for membership churn. To that end, similar to the discussion above, we characterize the membership churn in the steady state by the constant $\sigma = p_{pr}/(p_{pr} + p_{pf})$.

**Lemma 2.** *Let $\phi_I$ be the random variable representing the ratio of online voters for $A$ to online voters for $D$. In the steady state and for $\alpha \in (0, 1/2)$ it holds that*

$$
\Pr\left[\phi_I \geq \left(1 + \frac{2\alpha}{1 - \alpha}\right)s\right] < \left(\frac{\exp(\alpha)}{(1 + \alpha)^{1+\alpha}}\right)^{\sigma ns/(1+s)}
$$
$$
+ \left(\frac{\exp(-\alpha)}{(1 - \alpha)^{1-\alpha}}\right)^{\sigma n/(1+s)},
$$

*where $n$ is the cardinality of $I$, and $s$ is the ratio of $A$'s peers to $D$'s peers in $P$.*

The above lemma can be established using the same techniques as in the proof of Lemma 1. We therefore omit the proof here. Note that the parameter $s$ in Lemma 2 is directly affected by the outcome of the block mining process. Before establishing our main theorem we thus derive bounds on the miner's luck of the attacker in the following lemma.

**Lemma 3.** *Let $\phi_B$ be the random variable representing the ratio of $A$'s blocks to $D$'s blocks in the blockchain. In the steady state and for $\alpha > 0$ it holds that*

$$
\Pr[\phi_B \geq (1 + \alpha)t] \leq \left(\frac{\exp(\alpha)}{(1 + \alpha)^{1+\alpha}}\right)^{\ell t}
$$

*where $\ell$ is the current length of the blockchain, and $t$ is the fraction of $A$'s resources in $R$.*

*Proof.* Let $X_i$ be the 0/1 random variable indicating whether the attacker found block $i$, and let $X$ denote its sum. It holds that $E[X] = \ell t$, since the resource that found block $i$ is drawn uniformly at random from the online resources, and in the steady state a $t$-fraction of those belongs to $A$. By the Chernoff bound,

$$\Pr[X \geq (1 + \alpha)\ell t] \leq \left( \frac{\exp(\alpha)}{(1 + \alpha)^{1+\alpha}} \right)^{\ell t} .$$

Since $\ell\phi_B \geq X$, the probability of the event $\ell\phi_B \geq (1+\alpha)\ell t$ is upper bounded by the same term. Dividing by $\ell$ concludes the proof.                                                                     □

Note that the expected value of $\phi_B$ is not $t$—it rather depends on the resource distribution between $A$ and $D$. Suppose that $E[\phi_B] = u$, and set $\alpha = (u\alpha' - t + u)/t$ for some $\alpha' > 0$. Since $\alpha' > 0$ implies $\alpha > 0$, we may apply Lemma 3 to obtain the following technical corollary, which is the last building block for our proof of Theorem 1.

**Corollary 1.** *Let $\phi_B$ be the random variable representing the ratio of $A$'s blocks to $D$'s blocks in the blockchain. In the steady state and for $\alpha' > 0$ it holds that*

$$\Pr[\phi_B \geq (1 + \alpha')E[\phi_B]] \leq \left( \frac{\exp(\alpha)}{(1 + \alpha)^{1+\alpha}} \right)^{\ell t}$$

*where $\ell$ is the current length of the blockchain, $t$ is the fraction of $A$'s resources in $R$, and $\alpha = (E[\phi_B]\alpha' - t + E[\phi_B])/t$.*

### 4.4.2   Establishing Theorem 1

Let $\epsilon < 1/2$ be a positive constant. The goal is to show that if $\phi_R < 1/2 - \epsilon$, then with high probability the Chain Agreement is in a secure state. To that end, consider the complementary event **T** that the CA reaches an insecure state. We establish the claim by showing that **T** occurs with probability at most $\exp(-\Omega(\min(|R|, |I|, \ell)))$, where $R, I$, and $\ell$ are as above.

Let $\alpha, \beta, \gamma$ be positive constants with $\alpha + \beta + \gamma = \epsilon$. We would like to use Lemma 1, 2, and Corollary 1 to obtain the result. To apply those three we perform a worst case analysis: Consider the event $\mathbf{U}$ that after reaching the steady state, $\phi_R, \phi_B$, or $\phi_I$ deviate from their expected value by more than $\alpha, \beta$, or $\gamma$, respectively. Note that $\mathbf{U}$ occurring is necessary, but not sufficient, for $\mathbf{T}$ to occur.

Event $\mathbf{U}$ corresponds to the occurrence of at least one of the events bounded in Lemma 1, 2, and Corollary 1. Thus, applying the union bound to $\mathbf{U}$ yields

$$\begin{aligned} \Pr[\mathbf{T}] \leq \Pr[\mathbf{U}] \leq \quad &\Pr\left[\phi_R \geq (1+\alpha)\,E[\phi_R]\right] \\ &+ \Pr\left[\phi_B \geq (1+\beta)\,E[\phi_B]\right] \\ &+ \Pr\left[\phi_I \geq (1+\gamma)\,E[\phi_I]\right]. \end{aligned}$$

The statements of the two lemmas and the corollary can now be used to bound the three corresponding terms. This concludes our proof of Theorem 1. □

### 4.4.3 Reaching the Steady State

The security of the system hinges on it starting in a steady state, i.e., that there are a sufficient number of resources, voting identities and online peers. For example should no identity have been promoted yet, then the first block finder controls all identities in the system, trivially subverting the system. A bootstrapping period is used to ensure a large enough initial number of resources and voting identities set, resulting in good bounds on the failure probability. In order to reach a steady state it is necessary to bootstrap the system in a controlled way. Bootstrapping consists of determining a genesis block, an initial set of voting identities and an initial set of online identities.

PeerCensus can be bootstrapped by retrofitting the Bitcoin blockchain, providing the initial resources, blocks (voting identities) and peers. Every block in Bitcoin contains a *reward-transaction*, transferring a fixed amount of newly minted Bitcoins to the block finder. In order to receive the Bitcoins, the

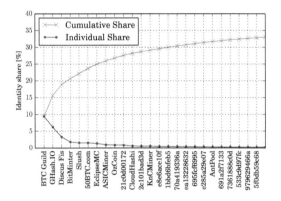

**Figure 4.4:** Bitcoin block finder distribution as of blockchain height 333,000 for the 25 most prominent mining pools.

block finder has to include a Bitcoin addresses in the transaction. This enables us to derive the new voting identity from the block by extracting the Bitcoin address from the reward transaction.

To migrate from Bitcoin to PeerCensus a migration time in the form of a blockchain length $l_m$ is determined in advance. Garay et al. [38] showed that with high probability peers agree on a common prefix, with distance $k$ from the current blockchain head and that the blockchain of length $j$ is a representative sample of online peers with high probability. Upon receiving a valid block for blockchain length $l_m$, peers extract the identities from blocks $[0, l_m - k]$. The Bitcoin genesis block is also the PeerCensus genesis block. The initial set of online identities is then assumed to consist of the last $j$ identities, i.e., the identities included in blocks $[l_m - k - j, l_m - k]$. The parameter $j$ should be chosen small enough so that $\lceil 2j/3 \rceil + 1$ identities are online to guarantee liveness, but large enough to ensure diversity in the entities. Once the set of voting and online voting identities are determined, peers start executing the

PeerCensus protocol. The peers then incrementally commit blocks at heights $[l_m - k, l_m]$.

The migration requires that in Bitcoin's current blockchain there is no entity that has mined a sufficient number of blocks to take control of the system. Fortunately, many mining pools include identifying hints in blocks, e.g., reusing the same address or including a text banner, so that the blocks can be attributed to the pool. This allows us to determine the block finder of a large percentage of blocks found so far in the blockchain. Figure 4.4 shows the current shares of blocks found by mining pools and therefore their share of identities in PeerCensus. Even if the largest 28 pools were to collaborate they would not reach a sufficient share of blocks to take control of the system. Furthermore, with $j \geq 10,000$ there is no single entity that controls more than 25% of identities, securing the migration itself.

So far we have not questioned the feasibility of large scale deployments of byzantine agreements. To sustain a high rate of operations, multiple operations should be batched and proposed at once. In a system with 25,000 peers and 10 second batches, each peer receives 3 messages per peer in the network every 10 seconds. Each message's size is dominated by the hash of the set of operations being voted on and the sending peer's signature, with 32 byte and 72 byte respectively. Each peer would have to send/receive approximately 780 kilobyte per second, which is below the average consumer bandwidth today.

### 4.4.4 Real World Guarantees

The previous subsections established that with high probability the system does not fail, for increasing number of resources and identities. In this section we give an example of the guarantees that are to be expected in real world instances of the PeerCensus system. In order to gauge the probability of a failure of the system we need to estimate some parameters used in the analysis.

For the resources we need to determine a maximum ratio of resources an attacker is allowed to control 25% which results in a security margin of $\epsilon = 1/2 - 1/3$. Notice that this is equivalent to the 13 largest mining pools colluding to subvert the system according to Figure 4.4. The number of resources is estimated as $1,000,000$, which at the current computational power in the Bitcoin network of $274,000,000 GH/s$ (Gigahashes) would mean that a unit resource has $274 GH/s$, which matches the currently available ASIC mining hardware. The number of blocks in the system is estimated as $350,000$ blocks, matching the Bitcoin blockchain length. The number of peers that are online in expectation is estimated at $25,000$ peers. Furthermore we adopt a conservative mean time between failures of 99 days and a mean time to recovery of 1 day for resources and peers, resulting in $\rho = \sigma = 0.99$. Applying Theorem 1 using these parameters yields the following upper bound on the failure probability of

$$\Pr[\text{PeerCensus is in a secure state}] \geq 1 - 4.26 \cdot 10^{-15}$$

in one time interval. Notice that this results from subdividing the security margin $\epsilon$ as $2\alpha_R = 14\%\epsilon$, $\alpha_M = 11\%\epsilon$ and $2\alpha_I = 75\%\epsilon$. If the system proceeds in discrete time intervals of 1 second, then the system therefore is expected to fail fewer than once every 7 million years.

## 4.5   Discoin

In the following we present Discoin, a cryptocurrency, as an exemplary application built on PeerCensus. Discoin tracks the balances of *accounts*, denominated in *coins*. An account $a$ is associated with a public-/private-keypair $(p_a, s_a)$. The public key $p_a$ is used to identify the account, while the private key $s_a$ is used to authenticate messages.

The shared state in Discoin consists of account balances $B$. In order to transfer coins between accounts we define a *transaction* $tx = \langle a, b, v \rangle_\sigma$. A transactions describes a transfer of $v$ coins from source account $a$ to destination account $b$ and includes signature $\sigma$ by the private key of $a$ to authorize the

---

**Specification:** Discoin Transaction processing

**Shared State:**
$\quad B \qquad\qquad \triangleright$ *Account balances*

**Validate** transaction($\langle a, b, v \rangle_\sigma$):
$\quad$ **if** $\sigma$ *is valid signature by* $s_a$ *and* $B[a] \geq v$ **then**
$\quad\quad$ **return** valid
$\quad$ **else**
$\quad\quad$ **return** invalid

**On Commit** transaction($\langle a, b, v \rangle_\sigma$):
$\quad B[a] \leftarrow B[a] - v$
$\quad B[b] \leftarrow B[b] + v$

---

**Figure 4.5:** Discoin protocol

transfer. A transaction is *valid* if the source account's balance $B[a] \geq v$, the signature $\sigma$ correctly signs $\langle a, b, v \rangle$ and matches the public key of $a$.

Discoin has a single operation transaction($tx$) which, if committed, applies the changes to the account balances. Upon committing a transaction($\langle a, b, v \rangle_\sigma$) operation the value is subtracted from the source account's balance and added to the destination account. Finally, Discoin distributes a reward of $r$ newly generated coins each time a block is found. The $r$ coins are distributed in equal parts to each identity $i \in I$. This reward is triggered by the timestamp change and does not necessitate a new transaction. By using PBFT we are guaranteed to process the transactions in the same order. The peers agree on the validity of individual transactions and on the current balance of each account.

Compared to Bitcoin, Discoin features a much leaner and simpler protocol. Unlike Bitcoin which tracks transaction outputs, we explicitly track account balances which results in a smaller shared state and a more intuitive concept of account balances. Committing a transaction is independent from the block generation and, more importantly, once transactions are committed they stay committed. By distributing rewards among all participants instead of just the block finder, Discoin continuously incentivizes peers to participate in the network. This contrasts Bitcoin's all-or-nothing rewards, which incentivize the creation of mining pools which pool resources and distribute the reward. Mining pools are seen as single points of failure in the Bitcoin ecosystem [36, 60, 76, 78].

As with the bootstrapping of PeerCensus, the accounts from Bitcoin can be migrated to Discoin. Once PeerCensus is bootstrapped, Discoin can be bootstrapped by computing the account address balances up to Bitcoin's blockchain height $l_m$. A snapshot of the balances is then committed before proceeding with the Discoin protocol and committing new transactions.

## 4.6   Related Work

The study of byzantine agreement protocols was initiated by the seminal works by Lamport et al. [51, 71], establishing tight feasibility results. PeerCensus and Discoin rely on byzantine agreement protocols that later improved message complexity, e.g., PBFT [25], Zyzzyva [50] and SGMP [74].

Bitcoin [68] is the latest, and most successful, in a long series of attempts to create a decentralized digital currency initiated by DigiCash [26] and ECash [27] by David Chaum. Recent work by Garay et al. [38] and Miller et al. [59] has shown that, with high probability, the peers participating in the Bitcoin network eventually agree on a transaction history. Reaching consistency however is a slow process as blocks are counted as individual votes for the validity of a transaction and confirmations are never final. Committing blocks in the CA resolves blockchain forks [30] early, rather than deferring the resolution to a later time, shown in [38] to be inefficient.

Today, a multitude of altcoins, i.e., alternative cryptocurrencies [58, 77] and so called Bitcoin 2.0 projects [23, 28, 86], are being used, each one using their own blockchain. This splits available resources and mining efforts, weakening the individual blockchains. Back et al. [13] proposed two-way pegged sidechains as a way to allow altcoins to be pegged to Bitcoin and to trade among altcoins, however each altcoin still has the burden of securing their own system via a blockchain.

Rosenfeld [76] analyses the difficulty of fairly distributing rewards among mining pool participants. Pools have become powerful entities often acting selfishly [10]. Eyal and Sirer [36] show that a mining pool may increase its share by not publishing blocks immediately. Miller [60] propose an alternative proof of work mechanism that would not allow pools to form.

Schwartz et al. [79] describe how consensus in Ripple is achieved by unique node lists assumed not to collude. Maintaining the node lists however requires manual configuration in order to avoid sybil attacks.

PeerCensus solves problems arising from inconsistent state views, such as double-spendings [14, 47]. It does not address problems like transaction malleability [31] and privacy issues, e.g., [6, 73].

## 4.7 Conclusion

We have presented a new system, PeerCensus, which enables strong consistency, forward security and commitment decoupled from the block rate for any number of application. The extensive analysis of the failure probability show that with high probability the system does not fail. Discoin, a digital cryptocurrency built on top of PeerCensus, is simpler to analyse and implement than the current Bitcoin system, provides stronger guarantees and faster confirmations.

# 5

# Duplex Micropayment Channels

Credit card companies process a growing number of transactions, currently more than 10,000 per second. In contrast, Bitcoin currently handles about one transaction per second. Bitcoin's turnover is growing, and ultimately Bitcoin may become a viable payment alternative. However, can Bitcoin scale to match the throughput of credit cards, or even an envisioned world of millions of micropayments per second?

The answer to this question is astonishingly negative. In order to verify whether a new transaction is valid, and in order to bootstrap new peers, every peer in the Bitcoin network stores every transaction ever. The size of an average transaction is 500 bytes, so with 1 transaction per second, every Bitcoin peer now needs almost 20 GB of additional storage each year. A turnover of 500 transactions per second would require 10 TB of additional disk space per year, which is at the limit for a consumer.

A bigger problem is processing power. Checking the signatures of each transaction (mostly because of disk seek time) takes about 5 ms, so with current machines we cannot hope to scale beyond 200 transactions per second.

Every node in the bitcoin network is informed about every transaction, multiple times because of the fault-tolerant gossip process. Assuming a common end-user bandwidth of 10 Mbit/s, then the rate peers can receive transactions is limited to approximately 1,000 transactions per second. Finally, while peers may individually be able to receive and process up to 200 transactions per second, the synchronization mechanism underlying Bitcoin is susceptible to latency, and does not work with transaction rates above 100 transactions per second [30].

In summary, Bitcoin in its current form will have a hard time scaling beyond 100 transactions per second, because of storage, processing, latency, and bandwidth. The problem of Bitcoin is its reliance on a synchronized global state, the replicated *blockchain*.

We propose to reduce the reliance on the blockchain to further decentralize the architecture of Bitcoin. We believe that the blockchain should only be used to establish long lived point-to-point channels between parties over which an arbitrary number of transfers can be performed. These transfers are no longer Bitcoin transactions that are committed to the blockchain, instead they rely on off-blockchain transactions that summarize any number of transfers between two parties. The blockchain is only involved during the setup and the closure of such a channel, while the vast majority of updates is never committed to the blockchain.

Towards this goal we present a duplex micropayment channel protocol. Duplex micropayment channels are established between *payment service providers* (PSPs). PSPs are the equivalent autonomous systems in the Internet, routing transfers between end users, possibly over multiple hops, guaranteeing end-to-end security and enabling real-time transfers. Unlike Bitcoin transactions, which take minutes to be confirmed, transfers over our duplex micropayment channels are final and can be accepted without further confirmations, enabling real-time payments, and a truly scalable future Bitcoin.

## 5.1 Bitcoin

In this section we give a short overview on the basic Bitcoin protocol. Specifics necessary for the duplex micropayment channel are discussed in detail later on. Bitcoin is a distributed system running on a homogeneous peer-to-peer network. Peers in the network collectively maintain a global state, known as the ledger, which tracks bitcoins and their associations. The fundamental data unit tracked by the network is the *output*, a tuple consisting of a value denominated in bitcoins and an output script. The output script sets up a claiming condition that has to be satisfied in order to claim the bitcoins associated with the output. The most common case is that a signature matching an address is required. Hence, the balance of an address is the sum of all outputs whose output scripts require that address' signature.

The only operation that may modify the global state is a *transaction*. A transaction claims one or more previously unclaimed outputs and creates new outputs. By providing inputs matching the output script, the creator of the transaction proves that she is allowed to claim the output. A transaction may redistribute the sum of values to new outputs and may set up arbitrary claiming conditions for the outputs.

In order to apply a transaction to the replicas of the ledger, the transaction is flooded in the network. When a node in the network receives a transaction the node first verifies the signatures of the transaction and, if valid, the transaction is applied to the local replica. For each input the script is executed with the input from the claiming transaction. If all scripts return true, the outputs were not claimed by a previous transaction, and the sum of new output values is smaller than the sum of claimed output values the transaction is valid. Due to the distributed nature of the system, the order in which transactions are applied is not identical across peers, and peers may disagree about the validity of a transaction, e.g., if two or more transactions attempt to claim the same output, the validity depends on the order they are seen by the peers.

Bitcoin eventually resolves inconsistencies by electing a peer as leader, which may then impose its changes to other peers, by sending a *block* containing all transactions it accepted since the last block. Each block contains a reference to its predecessor, incrementally building the *blockchain*, a shared history of all transactions that were applied. Transactions that are included in a block of the blockchain are said to be committed or confirmed. Leader election happens only rarely at random intervals; on expectation conflicts are resolved every 10 minutes. This is on purpose in order to minimize collisions in which multiple contradicting blocks are broadcast. However, it also introduces a long delay until a transaction is confirmed.

## 5.2 Building Blocks

In the following the concepts and sub-protocols used in this work are described in more detail.

### 5.2.1 Bitcoin Contracts

Off-blockchain transaction protocols are an example of *cryptocurrency contracts*. Contracts allow business logic to be encoded in Bitcoin transactions which mutually guarantee that an agreed upon action is performed. The blockchain acts as conflict mediator should a party fail to honor an agreement.

In this work we concentrate on off-blockchain transaction protocols. Furthermore we limit the description to two parties, $A$ and $B$, i.e., the two ends of the duplex micropayment channel. We denote the effective balances in the protocols or sub-protocols as $\sigma_A$ and $\sigma_B$. Since the balances may change we denote the balances after update $i$ as $\sigma_{A,i}$ and $\sigma_{B,i}$.

The main concern with off-blockchain transactions is to ensure that no party may renege on the agreement, possibly stealing funds from the other party. While on-blockchain transactions ascertain that a transaction has been committed before starting the next trade, a contract may last a long time and all parties have to ensure that they cannot be defrauded. A protocol is required in order to achieve mutual assurance that the latest update to the agreement is the one that will eventually be committed, and thus to invalidate any previous agreements. That is, each update creates a new set of transactions that supersede the previous update. At any time only one set of transactions may be released to Bitcoin and will be confirmed.

The protocol has to be carefully designed to avoid any possibility for fraud. Fraudulent behavior of a party may result in funds being stolen and funds being inaccessible either temporarily or permanently. Our protocol guarantees that funds are eventually refunded.

We assume that a suitable solution for transaction malleability [31] has been implemented [8, 87]. Since transactions refer to the outputs they spend by the hash of the transaction which created the output, any change causing the hash to change will unlink the transactions. The protocols in this work use chains of transactions with multiple signatures. Since ECDSA signatures are inherently malleable, anyone with the ability to re-sign a transaction may invalidate subsequent transactions. If deterministic and non-malleable signature schemes are used instead, all of our presented schemes can still be implemented securely, although they will become more complex. Most of the solutions aim to normalize transaction hashes by removing the signatures before hashing. This also enables the creation of transactions that spend outputs created by a transaction that is partially signed.

## 5.2.2 Timelocks and Invalidation

Bitcoin provides a mechanism to makes transactions invalid until some time in the future: *timelocks*. In addition to the validity conditions mentioned in the Section 5.1, a transaction may specify a locktime: the earliest time, expressed in either a Unix timestamp or a blockchain height, at which it may be included in a block and therefore be confirmed.

Peers in the network discard transactions with future timelocks. Any block including the transaction, that appears at a lower height or before the specified time, is deemed invalid. Timelocks can be used to replace or supersede transactions: a transaction with timelock $T$ can be superseded by another transaction, spending some of the same outputs, with timelock $T' < T$ and ensuring that the superseding transaction is broadcast to the network before the superseded transaction becomes valid.

Timelocks are transitive, i.e., a transaction spending an output created by a timelocked transaction will only be valid once the timelocked transaction is committed. Hence a transaction spending timelocked outputs has an effective timelock matching the maximum timelock of any transaction it depends on.

In order to update the contract, e.g., to increase the value one party will receive in the end, it is necessary to invalidate or replace transactions during the execution, ensuring that only the latest update is valid. Throughout the protocol two invalidation techniques are used:

- *Replace by timelock*: both parties hold fully signed transactions, with different bitcoin allocations, of which only one may be committed. All transactions have a timelock in the future. Only the transaction with the smallest timelock will eventually be committed, i.e., it is released before any other transaction becomes valid.

- *Replace by incentive*: one party has multiple fully signed transactions, with different values transferred to it, of which only one may be committed. The party will commit the transaction transferring the highest amount to it.

In order to guarantee that replace by timelock is secure the difference between timelocks that supersede each other has to be at least $\Delta T$. Due to the confirmation rate of Bitcoin we chose $\Delta T$ to be 1 hour. To simplify the notation we express timelocks as multiples of $\Delta T$ and use offsets such that the protocol starts at $T = 0$.

### 5.2.3 Shared Accounts

When an output can be claimed by providing a single signature it is called a *singlesig output*. In contrast the script of *multisig outputs* specifies a set of $n$ public keys and requires $m$-of-$n$ (with $m \leq n$) valid signatures from distinct matching public keys from that set in order to be valid.

In the 2-of-2 case two parties, $A$ and $B$, have to sign transactions spending the output. This is akin to a shared account where any transaction spending the common funds must be signed off by both parties. If both $A$ and $B$ have supplied $\sigma_A$ respectively $\sigma_B$ bitcoins to a multisig output, the output's value is $\sigma_A + \sigma_B$. Of this total value we say that $A$ effectively owns $\sigma_A$ and $B$ effectively owns $\sigma_B$, despite both signatures being required to spend the output.

Once a multisig output has been created and committed to the blockchain, $A$ and $B$ are guaranteed that the funds of the output may not be spent by either of the parties without both agreeing. As such the creation of a multisignature output is often used in order to setup a contract.

In order to securely create a shared account (multisig output) two transactions are needed: a *setup transaction* and a *refund transaction*. The setup transaction claims some funds from singlesig outputs owned by $A$ and $B$, and creates the multisig output. The refund transaction ensures that the funds are eventually refunded should one party disappear and not provide the necessary signatures to spend the multisig output.

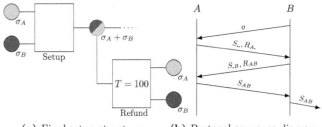

**(a)** Final setup structure.     **(b)** Protocol sequence diagram.

**Figure 5.1:** Setup creating a multisig output of value $\sigma_A + \sigma_B$ from two outputs of value $\sigma_A$ and $\sigma_B$. The refund transaction is timelocked and only valid after T=100. The sequence of transaction exchanges detailed on the right ensures the security of the setup. Subscripts represent the signatures by $A$ and $B$ or a . if a signature is missing.

Figure 5.1 shows the setup of a shared account coordinated by $A$. First $B$ sends a list $o$ of outputs it desires to add to the shared account, for a total value of $\sigma_B$ bitcoins. $A$ creates an unsigned setup transaction that claims both $o$ and its own outputs, with a value of $\sigma_A$ bitcoins, and creates a 2-of-2 multisig output requiring signatures from both $A$ and $B$ to be spent. In addition it creates a refund transaction that spends the newly created multisig output and transfers $\sigma_A$ to a singlesig output requiring $A$'s signature and $\sigma_B$ to a singlesig output requiring $B$'s signature. The refund transaction has a timelock some time in the future, making it invalid until that time.

The protocol sequence diagram in Figure 5.1 shows the order in which messages are exchanged. $A$ adds its signature to the refund transaction and sends both the refund transaction and the unsigned setup transaction to $B$. Upon receiving the transactions, $B$ verifies that the refund transaction eventually returns its funds and adds its signature to both transactions. $B$ now has a valid refund transaction and a partially signed setup transaction. Both transactions are returned to $A$ which adds the missing signature to the setup transaction, making all

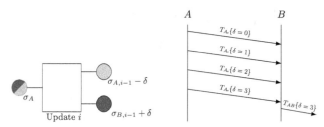

**(a)** Micropayment channel struc- **(b)** Payment channel sequence.
ture.

**Figure 5.2:** The structure of the payment channel consists of a single transaction splitting the value of a multisig output among the participants. In this case $A$ funded the channel and may send to $B$ and $\delta$ is the sum of increments.

transactions fully signed. The setup transaction is then released to the Bitcoin network and committed to the blockchain. This locks the funds until the refund returns them to the respective owners or until both parties agree on a different division of the funds, signing another transaction that supersedes the refund.

### 5.2.4 Simple Micropayment Channels

Simple micropayment channels first introduced by Hearn and Spilman [41] are contracts that can be established between two parties, a sender and a receiver. Once a micropayment channel is established, the sender can send incremental micropayments to the receiver. The channel has a limit determined by the sender upon the channel's creation. Once the limit is consumed, i.e., transferred entirely to the receiver, the channel is closed.

The micropayment channel can be created by setting up a shared account, as described in the previous section, between the sender and the receiver. The sender $A$ funds the channel with $\sigma_A$, whereas the receiver does not contribute, i.e., $\sigma_B$ is 0. We denote $\sigma_{A,i}$ and $\sigma_{B,i}$ to be the owned amounts after the $i^{th}$ update by $A$ and $B$ respectively.

In order to perform an incremental micropayment of value $\delta$ at time $i + 1$, $A$ creates a *micropayment update transaction* spending the multisig output and transferring $\sigma_{A,i+1} = \sigma_{A,i} - \delta$ and $\sigma_{B,i+1} = \sigma_{B,i} + \delta$ to $A$ and $B$ respectively.

The update transaction is signed by $A$ and sent to the receiver $B$. At this point the receiver could add its own signature and broadcast it to the Bitcoin network, committing it to the blockchain. However, normally the transaction is not broadcast. Instead the receiver accepts new update transactions, which transfer a larger amount to it. Only one of the update transactions may be committed to the blockchain since they all spend the same output. The receiver is incentivized to only use the latest update as it is the one paying out the maximum amount.

Eventually (i) all the initial funds $\sigma_{A,0}$ are transferred to $B$, (ii) both parties agree on closing the channel, or (iii) the refund time from the setup is approaching, triggering $B$ to close the channel. To close the channel, $B$ broadcasts the last update transaction which supersedes the refund transaction.

Note that such a micropayment channel is intrinsically unidirectional, i.e., the amount that the receiver is assigned in update transactions must be strictly increasing, otherwise the receiver might release an earlier update, which pays out a higher amount.

### 5.2.5 Atomic Multiparty Opt-In

In the shared account setup protocol, great care had to be taken about the order in which signatures were added, to avoid situations where funds could be locked in indefinitely. *Atomic multiparty opt-in* is an off-blockchain protocol that enables multiple parties to negotiate the creation of a complex structure of transactions, built on top of existing multisig outputs, without having to worry about the order in which the signatures are added. The structure can be negotiated openly since parties activate, or opt in, only after it is secure.

The atomic multiparty opt-in protocol uses an *opt-in trans-*

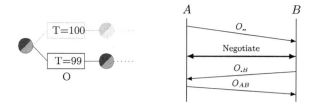

**Figure 5.3:** Opt-in structure to update an existing contract. The version on top is superseded by the lower version. Transactions attached to the root outputs on the right are negotiated openly, with the opt-in transaction determining validity.

*action* $O$ which claims a multisig output and creates a new multisig output, called the *root output*. Subsequent transactions spend the root output and thus are valid only if the opt-in transaction is valid, i.e., when all parties sign the opt-in transaction. This also obviates any refund addresses attached to intermediate outputs, which would be needed if each subsequent transaction were negotiated independently.

One party creates an unsigned opt-in transaction which spends a multisig output, requiring signatures from all participants, and creates one or more root outputs. The participants then collaborate to create the updated version of the contract, openly sharing any necessary transactions and signatures. As soon as all parties are content with the contract they sign the opt-in transaction, making it valid. The fully signed opt-in transaction is then exchanged among all participants to ensure that all parties can enforce the decision.

The atomic multiparty opt-in can be used in two ways: (i) to initially set up a contract starting from a multisig output owned by the participants, or (ii) to update an existing contract by building a structure that spends the root output of an outdated contract. In the latter case, depicted in Figure 5.3, it is necessary to enforce that only the new version is valid by using a smaller timelock.

The protocol is off-blockchain as its transactions are only

committed to the blockchain if one party defects. Notice that the party signing last may unilaterally decide whether to sign and commit or not. It is therefore advisable to use the multi-party opt-in exclusively in idempotent updates, i.e., when the value that is paid out to the parties does not change depending on whether or not the opt-in is committed.

### 5.2.6 Hashed Timelock Contracts (HTLC)

Hashed Timelock Contracts, or HTLCs, are contracts that require the recipient of a payment to reveal a secret in order to claim an output before it is refunded to the sender. The ability of the recipient to claim the output is therefore conditioned on its ability to reveal the secret.

This can be used to enable end-to-end security in a multi-hop scenario, in which a single payment is forwarded through multiple parties. In this scenario, $B$ requests a payment from $A$ and specifies the hash $h(S)$ of a secret $S$, which will be used to unlock the payment. $A$ creates an HTLC output from a shared account with the next hop on the path to $B$. The HTLC output sets up the claiming condition as shown in Figure 5.4: either the next hop provides $S'$ s.t. $h(S) = h(S')$ and a valid signature from both parties, or both parties must sign the transaction spending the HTLC output. This procedure is repeated by each node on the path until $B$ is reached. $B$ then releases $S$ to its previous node, claiming the HTLC output, and giving the previous node the ability to claim the previous HTLC output. This is repeated until the secret is revealed to $A$, thus completing the transfer.

For each hop there is a sender $H_A$ and a receiver $H_B$ and they share a multisig output that is used for the transfer. The HTLC output is created by an *HTLC setup transaction*, claiming the multisig output. During the execution of the protocol up to three transactions are created that may claim the HTLC output: a *refund transaction*, a *settlement transaction*, and a *forfeiture transaction*. The refund transaction is identical to the one from the shared account setup and ensures that $H_A$ is

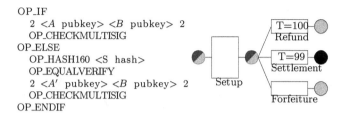

```
OP_IF
    2 <A pubkey> <B pubkey> 2
    OP_CHECKMULTISIG
OP_ELSE
    OP_HASH160 <S hash>
    OP_EQUALVERIFY
    2 <A' pubkey> <B pubkey> 2
    OP_CHECKMULTISIG
OP_ENDIF
```

**Figure 5.4:** HTLC output script and structure. The first branch is a normal multisig script while the second branch requires a secret and both signatures.

refunded should $H_B$ not cooperate. The settlement transaction performs the transfer from $H_A$ to $H_B$ if the latter reveals the secret. Finally, the forfeiture transaction is used to guarantee that $H_A$ is refunded even if the secret is eventually revealed. The last scenario is used to remove the HTLC output before the refund becomes valid, i.e., when both parties agree to free the funds locked in the HTLC output without performing the transfer.

The sender creates the HTLC setup transaction and all three transactions spending the HTLC output and signs refund transaction, forfeiture transaction and settlement transaction. The settlement transaction uses the *else*-branch of the script, which uses a separate *HTLC signing key* for the sender. This is necessary since otherwise $H_B$ could simply use the same signature in the *if*-branch, since signatures are valid for both branches. The partially signed refund, forfeiture and settlement transactions are then sent to the receiver which adds its signature to the refund and sends it back. The sender signs the HTLC setup transaction and sends it to the receiver, which may attempt to claim the HTLC output unilaterally by providing its signature and the secret to the settlement transaction.

The lifetime of the HTLC output is limited by the refund transaction's timelock, and should $H_B$ want to claim it, it must release the settlement transaction before the refund is valid. While this protocol works when committing transactions directly to the blockchain, its main use is in off-blockchain transactions.

In order to be usable in off-blockchain transactions, the timelock of the refund must be later than those in refund transactions attached to the root outputs, i.e., it must be guaranteed that $H_B$ indeed has time to claim the HTLC output on the blockchain before the refund transaction becomes valid. Should the receiver disclose the secret $S$ to the sender, then both parties can agree on removing the HTLC output and instead add its value to another output that directly transfers to the receiver. On the other hand, should $H_B$ not be able to disclose $S$ then it may decide to forfeit the HTLC output. In this case both parties sign the forfeiture transaction with no timelock, spending the HTLC output back to the sender. Once the sender has a fully signed forfeiture transaction, the receiver may not claim the HTLC output anymore since the forfeiture transaction is valid before the settlement transaction.

The HTLC output can be attached to an existing micropayment channel, the sender would simply send a micropayment update transaction which includes the HTLC output of value $\delta$.

## 5.3 Duplex Micropayment Channel

The secure setup, the micropayment channel and the hashed timelock contract alone enable the use multi-hop micropayments with end-to-end security. However setting up two independent micropayment channels between two peers, one for each direction between, is fairly limited. Each channel is unidirectional and is limited by the amount of bitcoins locked in during the setup by the sender. Once the limit has been consumed, the channel has to be torn down and a new one created, incurring time delay and cost of committing several transactions to the blockchain.

While this cannot be avoided on connections at the edge of the network in which a majority of payments flows in one direction, connections in which payments flow in both directions may take advantage from resetting their channels once the limit is consumed. For example, consider the channels $C_{AB}$ from $A$ to $B$ and $C_{BA}$ in the opposite direction, each initially funded with 1 coin. The limit of $C_{AB}$ may have been consumed, and $C_{BA}$ has a residual of 0.5 bitcoins. No further transfer from $A$ to $B$ can be performed despite $A$ having a non-zero balance on the $C_{BA}$ channel, i.e., when considering both channels the balances are $\sigma_A = 0.5$ and $\sigma_B = 1.5$. In order to enable future transfers from $A$ to $B$ both parties could agree to reset the channel, i.e., new channels $C'_{AB}$ and $C'_{BA}$ are created and funded with 0.5 and 1.5 bitcoins respectively. Notice that in both the depleted case and the reset case $A$ and $B$ own the same amount of bitcoins, but the channel their share is bound to has changed.

In the following we describe the duplex micropayment channel protocol that enables atomically resetting a set of channels. By doing so we enable the initial funds to be transferred over the duplex channel an arbitrary number of times, and hence reduce the necessity to commit to the blockchain.

A duplex micropayment channel (DMC) is established between two parties $A$ and $B$. The protocol establishes pairs of simple micropayment channels, one for each direction between the two parties. In order to reset the channels the protocol generates a sequence of pairs of unidirectional micropayment channels. We use $C_{AB,j}$ and $C_{BA,j}$ to indicate the simple micropayment channels in the $j^{th}$ pair of channels. Furthermore we define $\sigma_{X,j,i}$ to be the amount that the pair of micropayment channels would transfer to party $X \in \{A, B\}$ if they were committed to the blockchain after update $i$ in the pair $j$.

## 5.3.1 Structure

The fundamental structure of the DMC is the *invalidation tree*. The invalidation tree is a tree in which multisig outputs are the

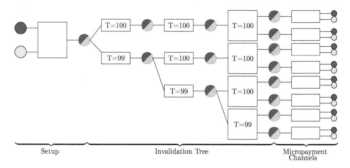

**Figure 5.5:** A full example of the duplex micropayment channel with $n = 1$ and $d = 3$, allowing up to 4 resets.

nodes of the tree, connected by transactions as edges. Each transaction in the tree is given a timelock, such that there is a unique minimal timelock among all sibling transactions, i.e., transactions sharing the same parent output. By the replace by timelock rule, only one path from the root of the tree is therefore first valid, i.e., the path with the minimal timelocks for each level in the tree. Hence as long as all timelocks are in the future, we can invalidate an entire subtree, by adding a new transaction spending that subtree's root output, with a smaller timelock than all existing transactions. We define two times $T_{max}$ and $T_{min}$ in terms of locktime. All refund transactions are set to have locktime $T_{max}$, forcing parties to commit the protocol's state to the blockchain before that time in order to avoid triggering the refunds. $T_{min}$ is the minimum timelock that is going to be used in the invalidation tree to replace other transactions. The time from the channel creation to $T_{min}$ is referred to as the channel's lifetime.

The number of replacement by timelock is limited by $n = (T_{max} - T_{min})/\Delta T$. Therefore each multisig output in the invalidation tree may have at most $n$ outgoing transactions which replace each other. Furthermore, due to the transitivity of timelocks, the full range may not be available as adding a timelock that is lower than one of its parent transactions has no effect: all transactions with a lower timelock become valid simultaneously, resulting in a race condition. For simplicity we limit the depth of the tree to $d$. This limits the number of transactions that have to be committed to the blockchain should one party defect.

The depth $d$, the number of replacements in the tree $n$ and time until funds are refunded $T_{max}$ are parameters to the duplex micropayment channel and are negotiated before the channel is created. $T_{min}$ can be derived from $T_{max}$, $n$ and $\Delta T$, which is a system parameter.

Furthermore, knowing $n$ and $d$ allows the enumeration of all branches in the tree. A branch can be represented as a string of length $d$, the alphabet $\{T_{min}, ..., T_{max}\}$ and the elements are increasing. Thus every branch has a unique successor that directly invalidates it. This facilitates the negotiation of which branch to select next.

The internal nodes of the invalidation tree are individual multisig outputs, while the leafs of the tree are pairs of multisig outputs. On the leaf outputs a pair of simple micropayment channels is built, one transferring from $A$ to $B$ and the other one in the opposite direction.

Multi-hop payment flows result in HTLC outputs being attached to the simple micropayment channel matching the direction of the flow. The timelock of the transactions spending the HTLC outputs are larger than $T_{max}$. This ensures that the micropayment channel creating the HTLC have been committed to the blockchain and replace by timelock can be performed. The period between $T_{max}$ and the last HTLC output being claimed is referred to as *conflict resolution phase*.

## 5.3.2 Setup

The setup initiates the micropayment channel between two parties by locking in the initial funds into a shared account. The shared account creation subprotocol from Section 5.2.3 is used to create the multisig output. Both parties exchange a set of singlesig outputs they would like to contribute to the channel and create the setup transaction. The initial funds from $A$ and $B$ are denoted as $\sigma_{A,0,0}$ and $\sigma_{B,0,0}$ since there were no resets and no updates yet. The refund transaction has a timelock of $T_{max}$. It transfers the funds back to their owners if no other agreement is committed first. Since the setup transaction is committed in the blockchain it is safe to build upon the multisig output. Committing the transaction may take several minutes and the channel is not operational until it is committed.

### 5.3.3  Reset

The reset process takes care of building a new branch of the invalidation tree and setting up the micropayment channels. This includes the first branch starting from the shared account the setup created. A reset is triggered after the initial setup, as well as when the limit of one of the simple micropayment channels is depleted. Assuming that the limit of $A$'s channel $C_{AB,j}$ is consumed and therefore requires a reset. $A$ is said to coordinate the reset: it will no longer perform updates to its channel $C_{AB,j}$ and send a *reset request* to the $B$. Upon receiving the reset request, $B$ stops performing updates to its channel $C_{BA,j}$ and sends a *reset response*. The reset response signals to $A$ that $B$ is willing to perform the reset and that no further updates to $C_{BA,j}$ will be performed and that the value transferred by the two simple micropayment channels $\sigma_{A,j,i}$ and $\sigma_{B,j,i}$ will not change.

Upon receiving the reset response, $A$ can proceed to build the next branch ending in two multisig outputs. The values of the two multisig outputs are $\sigma_{A,j+1,0} = \sigma_{A,j,i}$ and $\sigma_{B,j+1,0} = \sigma_{B,j,i}$, i.e., each multisig output is virtually owned by one party and its value represents the share the owner would get if the current branch were to be committed. On top of the leaf multisig outputs two new simple micropayment channels $C_{AB,j+1}$ and $C_{BA,j+1}$ are built with respective refund transactions. The branch is negotiated as an instance of the atomic multiparty opt-in protocol, with the transaction spending the existing output from the previous branch as opt-in transaction and the remainder of the branch as subsequent structure. $A$ may sign the entire branch where necessary, except the opt-in transaction, which may only be signed once $B$ has signed the refund transactions for the simple micropayment channels, therefore assuring that funds will not be locked in indefinitely.

The atomic multiparty opt-in ensures that either both agree on switching to the new branch or the old branch remains active. In both cases the same amounts are transferred to the two parties and updates to the micropayment channels $C_{AB,j+1}$ and $C_{BA,j+1}$ resume only once both parties have a fully signed opt-in transaction.

### 5.3.4 Teardown and Commit

Eventually the duplex micropayment channel needs to be closed and the summary of the channel committed to the blockchain. The closure of the duplex micropayment channel can be triggered by agreement or by the end to the channel's lifetime. Either both parties agree on the summary, or they disagree and do not collaborate. In the first case they may simply create a *teardown transaction*, which transfers $\sigma_{A,j,i}$ to $A$ and $\sigma_{B,j,i}$ to $B$, assuming update $i$ is the latest update in the current round $j$. The teardown transaction is not timelocked and directly spends the multisig output created in the setup process, hence it can be committed to the blockchain immediately. The process simply involves one party creating the teardown transaction, both parties signing it and committing it to the blockchain. HTLC outputs which have not been removed by agreement can be copied over to the summary transaction such that the same timelocks and resolution rules apply.

In the case parties do not agree on the summary of the channel, they still have the latest branch of the invalidation tree that guarantees eventual conflict resolution. Before the refunds become valid the branch is submitted to the Bitcoin network and will be committed to the blockchain. Unlike the commit using a summary transaction, which requires just a single transaction to be committed, the resolution by tree branch requires up to $d + 2$ transactions, hence we limit on the depth of the tree.

### 5.3.5 Refresh

In the case two parties have an existing duplex micropayment channel its lifetime may be extended using the refresh process. Analogously to the reset sub-protocol, both parties stop updating the existing duplex micropayment channel by exchanging *refresh request* and *refresh response* messages, thus flushing pending changes. The parties agree on new parameters $T_{max}$ and $T_{min}$ determining the new channel's lifetime. One party creates an opt-in transaction creating a new root output and a refund transaction with a timelock of $T_{max}$ transferring $\sigma_{A,j,i}$ and $\sigma_{B,j,i}$ to their respective owners. Both parties then perform the atomic multiparty opt-in protocol using the opt-in transaction and the refund as subsequent structure. The opt-in transaction is then published on the Bitcoin network and committed to the blockchain, invalidating the entire invalidation tree built on the old root output.

Special care has to be taken with HTLC outputs as these may time out during the new channel's lifetime. The HTLC outputs are copied over to the opt-in transaction, and their resolution is handled on the blockchain.

The refreshed duplex micropayment channel is operational immediately, since the opt-in transaction is guaranteed to be eventually confirmed, i.e., no party may double-spend the old root output.

In addition funds can be removed and added during the refresh process. Funds can be removed adding singlesig outputs to the opt-in transaction that pay out part of a party's balance to one of its addresses, that party's share of the channel is then reduced accordingly. In order to add funds to the channel, a multisig output owned by both parties has to be created ahead of time using the protocol in Section 5.2.3 so that during the refresh the outputs are committed to the blockchain. This multisig output is then also claimed by the opt-in.

## 5.4 Routing Payments

A channel between two payment service providers (PSPs) can be established once; it has a lifetime of hundreds of days before it is either torn down or refreshed. The setup requires a single transaction that is committed to the blockchain locking in the initial funds, while the teardown requires a single transaction committed to the blockchain. In the case the two parties do not collaborate to close the channel, at most $d$ transactions from the invalidation tree and two micropayment updates have to be committed to the blockchain. The amount of bitcoins transferred is only limited by the number of resets and the initial funds parties contribute to the channel. A channel with $n = 46$ and $d = 11$ results in $1.48 \cdot 10^{11}$ resets. If such a channel is initially funded with 1 bitcoin, the channel can be used to transfer a total of 148 billion bitcoins, an equivalent of 35.3 trillion USD at today's exchange rate, twice the US national debt. Notice that both $n$ and $d$ can be chosen arbitrarily, further extending the amount transferable by a channel.

By adding HTLC outputs to the micropayment channels, instead of sending the increment directly, the payment can be end-to-end secured so that the recipient of a payment has to confirm reception. The final recipient communicates the secret out of band to the sender of the payment. Each hop along the route from the sender to the recipient will create HTLC outputs transferring the funds only upon receiving the secret, which is only released once the final recipient is assured that the total is transferred.

## 5.5 Related Work

Bitcoin was introduced by Nakamoto in 2008 [68] and has since enjoyed a rapid growth both in value as in transaction volume. However, the design of Bitcoin intrinsically limits the rate it can process transactions. Barber et al. [15] identified problems with data retention, which later were adopted to create the simplified payment verification, using filtering nodes for mobile clients. An analysis of the information propagation [30] showed that the probability of blockchain forks rapidly increases with increasing transaction rates and the eventually the network is no longer able to resolve conflicts. Eyal et al. [36] further show how miners may use the propagation delay in the network as a force multiplier.

The GHOST protocol [80] allows an increase of the block generation rate by reusing blocks that are not in the main blockchain. Although mainly aimed at enabling innovation, Back et al. [13] propose dividing the single Bitcoin network into smaller networks that can operate independently. Discoin and PeerCensus [29] decouple the confirmation of transactions from the block generation and guarantee strong consistency. The slow confirmation also prevents a number of real-life uses of Bitcoin, as fast payment can be double-spent and not be detected for some time [14, 47, 78]. Our proposal enables secure end-to-end payments that do not require being confirmation in the blockchain, hence enabling true micropayment that clear in real-time.

Simple micropayment channels were introduced by Hearn et al. [41]. Finally the Lightning Network by Poon and Dryja [72], also creates a duplex micropayment channel. However it requires exchanging keying material for each update in the channels, which results in either massive storage or computational requirements in order to invalidate previous transactions. In our proposal the two channels operate independently allowing fully asynchronous operation between resets. Lightning renews the whole transaction structure on every update, requiring synchronous updates and high bandwidth consumption. Furthermore the Lightning protocol cannot be decomposed into smaller units that can be analyzed in isolation, making the security analysis difficult and resulting in complex implementations.

## 5.6 Conclusion

Duplex micropayment channels solve a multitude of problems. For one they enable near-infinite scalability for digital payments based on Bitcoin. Bitcoin transactions are no longer used directly to transfer bitcoins from a sender to a recipient, instead they are used to setup micropayment channels and handle conflict resolution. The actual transfers are now handled at a higher level through a network of payment service providers. The payments are end-to-end secure thanks to the use of hashed timelock contracts, ensuring transfers between hops are only performed if the intended recipient receives its payment. Unlike Bitcoin, which requires a long confirmation process, transfers on a network of duplex micropayment channels are secure from being reverted. Thus a payment network using duplex micropayment channels is a far better fit for real-time scenarios, e.g., buying a coffee, since transfers can be performed at the same speed messages are passed in the Internet. With a network of payment service providers, Bitcoin can support true micropayments with minimal fees at unprecedented scale, and where the transfers clear in real-time.

# 6

# Transaction Malleability and MtGox

In recent years Bitcoin [68] has gone from a little experiment by tech enthusiasts to a global phenomenon. The cryptocurrency is seeing a rapid increase in adoption as well as in value. Bitcoin is inching closer to the stated goal of creating a truly decentralized global currency that facilitates international trade.

A major contribution of the success that Bitcoin is having today has to be attributed to the emergence of Bitcoin exchanges. A Bitcoin exchange is a platform that facilitates buying and selling bitcoins for fiat money like US dollars. This enables a larger public to come in contact with bitcoins, increasing their value as a means to pay for goods and services. Exchanges also provide the ground truth for the value of bitcoins by publishing their trade book and allowing market dynamics to find a price for the traded bitcoins. Finally, much of the media attention focuses on the rapid gain in value that these services have enabled.

However, centralized exchanges are also potential points of failure, in a system that is otherwise completely decentralized. Several high value thefts from these services have made the headlines, never failing to predict the impending doom of Bitcoin as a whole. Additionally a small and mostly sentiment driven market, combined with a quick and easy way to buy and sell bitcoins, facilitates flash crashes and rapid rallies for no apparent reason.

The first, and for a long time largest, Bitcoin exchange was MtGox. Founded in 2010 it was a first stop for many early adopters. With the creation of other exchanges its monopoly slowly faded, but in February 2014 it still accounted for close to 70% of all bitcoins ever traded. In February 2014 MtGox had to file for bankruptcy and suspend operations following the loss of over 500 million USD worth of bitcoins owned by its customers.

As the principal cause for the loss, MtGox cited a problem in the Bitcoin protocol: *transaction malleability*. A user could request a withdrawal from MtGox to a Bitcoin address. The exchange would then create a corresponding transaction and publish it to the Bitcoin network. Due to the way MtGox tracked confirmation of these transactions it could be tricked, exploiting transaction malleability, into believing the transaction to have failed even though it was later confirmed by the network. MtGox would then credit the amount back to the user's account. Effectively the user would have doubled the withdrawn bitcoins, once from the withdrawal and once on its account on MtGox.

In this chapter we investigate two fundamental questions: Is transaction malleability being exploited? And is the claim that it has been used to bring down MtGox plausible?

## 6.1 Transaction Malleability

The Bitcoin network is a distributed network of computer nodes controlled by a multitude of owners. They collectively implement a replicated ledger that tracks the address balances of all users. Each user may create an arbitrary number of addresses that can be used to send and receive bitcoins. An address is derived from an ECDSA key pair that is later used to prove ownership of the bitcoins associated with that address.

The only operation allowed to modify address balances are *transactions*. A transaction is a signed data structure that on the one hand claims some bitcoins associated with a sending address and on the other hand reassigns them to receiving addresses. Transactions are identified by the SHA256 hash of their serialized representation. A transaction consists of one or more *inputs* and an ordered list of one or more *outputs*. An input is used to specify which bitcoins will be transferred, while an output specifies the address that should be credited with the bitcoins being transferred. Formally, an output is a tuple comprising the value that is to be transferred and a *claiming condition*, expressed in a simple scripting language. An input includes the hash of a previous transaction, an index, and a *claiming script*. The hash and index form a reference that uniquely identifies the output to be claimed and the claiming script proves that the user creating the transaction is indeed the owner of the bitcoins being claimed.

### 6.1.1 Bitcoin Scripts

The scripting language is a, purposefully non-Turing complete, stack-based language that uses single byte opcodes. The use of the scripting language to set up both the claiming conditions and the claiming scripts allows the creation of complex scenarios for the transfer of bitcoins. For example, it is possible to create multi-signature addresses that require $m$-of-$n$ signatures to spend the associated bitcoins for arbitration purposes. However, the vast majority of transactions use standard scripts that set up a claiming condition requiring the claiming script to provide a public key matching the address and a valid signature of the current transaction matching the public key. For this reason the standard claiming script is generally referred to as *scriptSig* (a script encoding a signature), whereas the standard claiming condition is referred to as *scriptPubKey* (a script requiring a public key and a signature). Figure 6.1 shows the structure of the standard claiming condition (scriptPubKey) as well as the standard claiming script (scriptSig).

Of particular interest in this work are the OP_PUSHDATA operations which specify a number of following bytes to be pushed as a string on the stack. Depending on the length of the string one of several possible flavors may be used. The simplest is a single byte with value between $0x00$ and $0x4b$, also called OP_0 which simply encodes the length of the string in itself. Additionally, three other operations allow pushing data on the stack, namely OP_PUSHDATA1, OP_PUSHDATA2 and OP_PUSHDATA4, each followed by 1, 2 or 4 bytes, respectively, encoding a little endian number of bytes to be read and pushed on the stack.

In order to verify the validity of a transaction $t_1$ claiming an output of a previous transaction $t_0$ the scriptSig of $t_1$ and the scriptPubKey specified in $t_0$ are executed back to back, without clearing the stack in between. The scriptSig of $t_1$ pushes the signature and the public key on the stack. The scriptPubKey of $t_0$ then duplicates the public key (OP_DUP) and replaces the first copy with its RIPEMD160 hash (OP_HASH160), this 20 byte derivative of the public key is also encoded in the address. The address from the scriptPubKey is then pushed on the stack and the two top elements are then tested for equality (OP_EQUALVERIFY). If the hash of the public key and the expected hash match, the script continues, otherwise execution is aborted. Finally, the two elements remaining on the stack, i.e., the signature and the public key, are used to verify that the signature signs $t_1$ (OP_CHECKSIG).

Notice that, although the scriptSigs are attached to the inputs of the transaction, they are not yet known at the time

**Listing 6.1:** scriptPubKey

```
OP_DUP
OP_HASH160
OP_PUSHDATA*
<pubKeyHash>
OP_EQUALVERIFY
OP_CHECKSIG
```

**Listing 6.2:** scriptSig

```
OP_PUSHDATA*
<sig>
OP_PUSHDATA*
<pubKey>
```

**Figure 6.1:** The standard claiming condition and claiming script as used by simple transactions transferring bitcoins to an address backed by a single public key.

the signature is created. In fact a signature may not sign any data structure containing itself as this would create a circular dependency. For this reason all the claiming scripts are set to a script consisting only of a single OP_0 that pushes an empty string on the stack. The user signing the transaction then iterates through the inputs, temporarily replaces the scriptSig field with the corresponding scriptPubKey[1] from the referenced output, and creates a signature for the resulting serialized transaction. The signatures are then collected and inserted at their respective positions before broadcasting the transaction to the network.

The fact that the integrity of the scriptSig cannot be verified by the signature is the source for transaction malleability: the claiming script may be encoded in several different ways that do not directly invalidate the signature itself. A simple example replaces the OP_0 that pushes the public key on the stack with OP_PUSHDATA2 followed by the original length. The claiming script is changed from 0x48<sig>41<pubKey> to 0x4D4800<sig>4D4100<pubKey>. The encoded signature is valid in both cases but the hash identifying the transaction is different.

---

[1]The use of the scriptPubKey in the signed data as placeholder for the scriptSig is likely to avoid collisions.

Besides these changes in the way pushes are encoded, there are numerous sources of malleability in the claiming script. A Bitcoin Improvement Proposal (BIP) by Wuille [87] identifies the following possible ways to modify the signature and therefore exploit malleability:

1. ECDSA signature malleability: signatures describe points on an elliptic curve. Starting from a signature it is trivial to mathematically derive a second set of parameters encoding the same point on the elliptic curve;

2. Non-DER encoded ECDSA signatures: the cryptographic library used by the Bitcoin Core client, OpenSSL, accepts a multitude of formats besides the standardized DER (Distinguished Encoding Rules) encoding;

3. Extra data pushes: a scriptPubKey may push additional data at the beginning of the script. These are not consumed by the corresponding claiming condition and are left on the stack after script termination;

4. The signature and public key may result from a more complex script that does not directly push them on the stack, but calculates them on the fly, e.g., concatenating two halves of a public key that have been pushed individually;

5. Non-minimal encoding of push operations: as mentioned before there are several options to specify identical pushes of data on the stack;

6. Zero-padded number pushes: excessive padding of strings that are interpreted as numbers;

7. Data ignored by scripts: if data pushed on the stack is ignored by the scriptPubKey, e.g., if the scriptPubKey contains an OP_DROP, the corresponding push in the scriptSig is ignored;

8. Sighash flags can be used to ignore certain parts of a script when signing;

9. Any user with access to the private key may generate an arbitrary number of valid signatures as the ECDSA signing process uses a random number generator to create signatures;

## 6.1.2 Malleability Attacks

One of the problems that Bitcoin sets out to solve is the problem of *double spending*. If an output is claimed by two or more transactions, these transactions are said to *conflict*, since only one of them may be valid. A *double spending attack* is the intentional creation of two conflicting transactions that attempt to spend the same funds in order to defraud a third party.

Research so far has concentrated on a classical version of the double spending attack. An attacker would create two transactions: (1) a transaction that transfers some of its funds once to a vendor accepting bitcoins and (2) a transaction that transfers those same funds back to itself. The goal would then be to convince the vendor that it received the funds, triggering a transfer of goods or services from the vendor to the attacker, and ensuring that the transaction returning the funds to the attacker is later confirmed. This would defraud the vendor as the transfer to the vendor would not be confirmed, yet the attacker received the goods or services.

A *malleability attack*, while a variant of the double spending attack, is different from the above. The attacker no longer is the party issuing the transaction, instead it is the receiving party. The attacker would cause the victim to create a transaction that transfers some funds to an address controlled by the attacker. The attacker then waits for the transaction to be broadcast in the network. Once the attacker has received a copy of the transaction, the transaction is then modified using one of the above ways to alter the signature without invalidating it. The modification results in a different transaction identification hash. The modified transaction is then also broadcast in the network. Either of the two transactions may later be confirmed.

A malleability attack is said to be successful if the modified version of the transaction is later confirmed. The mechanics of how transactions are confirmed are complex and are out of scope for this work. For our purposes it suffices to say that the probability of a malleability attack to be successful depends on the distribution of nodes in the Bitcoin network first seeing either of the transactions (cf. [14, 30, 47]). So far the attack has not caused any damage to the victim. To be exploitable the victim also has to rely solely on the transaction identity hash to track and verify its account balance. Should a malleability attack be successful the victim will only see that the transaction it issued has not been confirmed, crediting the amount to the attacker or attempting to send another transaction at a later time. The attacker would have effectively doubled the bitcoins the victim sent it.

It is worth noting that the reference client (Bitcoin Core) is not susceptible to this attack as it tracks the unspent transaction output set by applying all confirmed transactions to it, rather than inferring only from transactions it issued.

## 6.2   MtGox Incident Timeline

In this section we briefly describe the timeline of the incident that eventually led to the filing for bankruptcy of MtGox. The timeline is reconstructed from a series of press release by MtGox as well as the official filings and legal documents following the closure.

Following several months of problems with Bitcoin withdrawals from users, MtGox announced [67] on February 7 that it would suspend bitcoin withdrawals altogether. The main problem with withdrawals was that the associated Bitcoin transactions would not be confirmed. After this press release it was still possible to trade bitcoins on MtGox, but it was not possible to withdraw any bitcoins from the exchange. Specifically [67] does not mention transaction malleability.

In order to trade on MtGox, users had transferred bitcoins and US dollars to accounts owned by MtGox. Each user would have a virtual account that is credited with the transferred amounts at MtGox. The withdrawal stop therefore denied users access to their own bitcoins. While fiat currency was still withdrawable, such a withdrawal involved a long process that would sometimes fail altogether.

The first press release was followed by a second press release [66] on February 10, 2014. This press release claims that the problem for the non-confirming withdrawal transactions has been identified and names transaction malleability as the sole cause:

> "Addressing Transaction Malleability: MtGox has detected unusual activity on its Bitcoin wallets and performed investigations during the past weeks. This confirmed the presence of transactions which need to be examined more closely.
>
> Non-technical Explanation: A bug in the bitcoin software makes it possible for someone to use the Bitcoin network to alter transaction details to make it seem like a sending of bitcoins to a bitcoin wallet did not occur when in fact it did occur. Since the transaction appears as if it has not proceeded correctly, the bitcoins may be resent. MtGox is working with the Bitcoin core development team and others to mitigate this issue."

Allegedly a user of MtGox would request a withdrawal and listen for the resulting transaction. The transaction would then be intercepted and replaced by a modified version that would then race with the original transaction to be confirmed. Should the original transaction be confirmed, the user would receive its balance only once, but not lose any bitcoins by doing so. Should the modified transaction be confirmed, then the user would receive the bitcoins twice: once via the modified withdrawal transaction and a second time when MtGox realized that the original withdrawal transaction would not confirm and credit the users account. Implicitly in this press release MtGox admits to using a custom client that tracks transaction validity only via its hash, hence being vulnerable to the transaction malleability attack.

Two more press releases followed on February 17 and February 20, both claiming that the withdrawals would resume shortly and that a solution had been found that would eliminate the vulnerability to malleability attacks. On February 23 the website of MtGox returned only a blank page, without any further explanation, resulting in a trading halt and the complete disappearance of MtGox. Finally on February 28 MtGox announced during a press conference that it would be filing for bankruptcy in Japan and in the USA [64, 65].

## 6.3   Measurements

Due to the nature of double spending attacks, they may only be detected while participating in the network. As soon as one of the two conflicting transactions is considered to be confirmed the nodes will drop all other conflicting transactions, losing all information about the double spending attack. Malleability attacks being a subset of double spending attacks suffer from the same limitation.

We created specialized nodes that would trace and dump all transactions and blocks from the Bitcoin network. These include all double spending attacks that have been forwarded to any of the peers our nodes connected to. Our collection of transactions started in January 2013. As such we are unable to reproduce any attacks before January 2013. The following observations therefore do not consider attacks that may have happened before our collection started.

Our nodes were instructed to keep connection pools of 1,000 connections open to peers in the Bitcoin network. On average we connected to 992 peers, which at the time of writing is approximately 20% of the reachable nodes. According to Bamert et al. [14] the probability of detecting a double spending attack quickly converges to 1 as the number of sampled peers increases. We therefore feel justified in assuming that the transactions collected during the measurements faithfully reflect the double spending attacks in the network during the same period.

## 6.3.1 Global Analysis

Given the set of all transactions, the first task is to extract all potential double spend attacks. In general double spending attacks can be identified by associating a transaction with each output that it claims. Should there be more than one transaction associated with the same output the transactions conflict. The malleability attack being a specialized case of the double spend attack could also be identified by this generic procedure, however we opted for a simpler process. Removing the signature script from a transaction results in the signed part of the transaction, forcing all malleability attacks to produce the same unique key. The unique key is then used to group transactions together into *conflict sets*.

During the measurement period a total of 35,202 conflict sets were identified, each evidence of a malleability attack. Out of these conflict sets 29,139 contained a transaction that would later be confirmed by a block. The remaining 6,063 transactions were either invalid because they claimed non-existing outputs, had incorrect signatures, or they were part of a further double spending.

The *conflict set value* is defined as the number of bitcoins transferred by any one transaction in the conflict set. The outputs of the transactions in a conflict set are identical, since any change to them would require a new signature. In particular the value of outputs may not be changed. Each transaction in a conflict set therefore transfers an identical amount of bitcoins. Summing the value of all conflict sets results in a total of 302,700 bitcoins that were involved in malleability attacks.

As mentioned in Section 6.1.1, there are a multitude of ways to use the malleability in the signature encoding to mount a malleability attack. The most prominent type of modification was replacing the single byte OP_0 with OP_PUSHDATA2 which then encodes the length of the data to push on the stack with 2 bytes. The resulting signature script would be 4 bytes longer, because two strings are usually pushed on the stack, but would still encode the same DER encoded signature and the same public key, hence still be valid. A total of 28,595 out of the 29,139 confirmed attacks had this type of modifications. For the remaining 544 conflict sets we were unable to identify the original transactions. All transactions in these conflict sets had genuine signatures with the correct opcodes and did not encode the same signature. We therefore believe these transactions to be the result of users signing raw transactions multiple times, e.g., for development purposes.

In order for a malleability attack to be exploitable two conditions have to be fulfilled: (a) the modified transaction has to be later confirmed and (b) the system issuing the transaction must rely solely on the transaction's original hash to track its confirmation. The first condition can be easily reconstructed from the network trace and the Bitcoin blockchain since only one of the transactions will be included in the blockchain. The second condition is not detectable in our traces since it depends on the implementation of the issuing system. In particular, it is not possible to determine whether two payments with the same value to the same address were intended as two separate payments or whether an automated system issued the second one believing the first to be invalid.

We call a malleability attack successful if it resulted in the modified transaction to be later confirmed in a block, i.e., when condition (a) holds. From the data derived from the attack classification we can measure the rate of successful malleability attacks. Out of the 28,595 malleability attacks that used an OP_PUSHDATA2 instead of the default OP_0 only 5,670 were successful, i.e., 19.46% of modified transactions were later confirmed. Considering the value in malleable transactions the success rate is comparable with 21.36%. This reduces the total profit of the successful attacks from 302,700 to 64,564. The strong bias towards the original transaction is explained by the fact that the probability of being confirmed depends on the distribution of the transaction in the network [14]. During a malleability attack the attacker listens for an incoming transaction that match its address, modifies it and redistributes it. In the meantime however the original transaction has been further forwarded in the network and the modified transaction is not forwarded by nodes seeing the original transaction. The attacker must connect to a large sample of nodes in the network for two reasons: (a) intercept the original transaction as soon as possible and (b) compensate the head start that the original transaction has compared to the modified transaction.

So far we assumed that the conflict sets were a direct result of a targeted attack by an attacker against a service. There are however other causes for this kind of conflict that should not go unmentioned. An automated system may inadvertently create, sign a transaction and broadcast a transaction multiple times. Due to a random parameter in the signing process the system would produce a different signature each time, causing the conflict that we detected. This appears to be the case with transactions having conflict set cardinality larger than 2, that would often not be confirmed.

## 6.3.2 The MtGox Incident

Returning to the specific case of the MtGox incident of February 2014, that eventually lead to the closure and the bankruptcy filing later that same month. In the press release of February 10, the transaction malleability bug was explicitly named as the root cause of the loss. The loss is later detailed as amounting to over 850,000 bitcoins, of which 750,000 bitcoins were customer owned bitcoins that were managed by MtGox. At the time of the first press release bitcoins were trading at 827 US Dollars per bitcoin,[2] resulting in a total value of lost bitcoins of 620

---

[2] Exchange rate taken as the open value on MtGox of February 7, 2014.

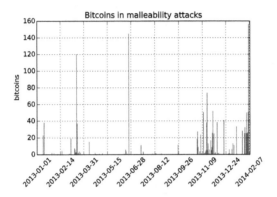

**Figure 6.2:** Malleability attacks during period 1, before the press release blaming transaction malleability as the sole cause of losses.

million US Dollars.

Assuming malleability attacks hav indeed been used to defraud MtGox, then we should be able to verify the claim by finding the transactions used for the attack in our dataset. The above mentioned total amount of 302,700 bitcoins involved in malleability attacks already disproves the existence of such a large scale attack. However, it could well be that malleability attacks contributed considerably in the declared losses.

Reconstructing the timeline of the attacks from the announcements made by MtGox we identify 3 time periods:

- Period 1 (January 2013 — February 7, 2014): over a year of measurements until the closure of withdrawals from MtGox;

- Period 2 (February 8 — February 9, 2014): withdrawals are stopped but no details about the attack known to the public;

- Period 3 (February 10 — February 28): time following the press release blaming transaction malleability as the

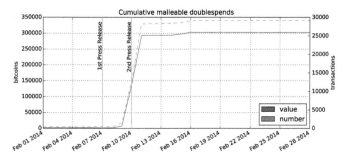

**Figure 6.3:** Cumulative graph of the number and value of malleability attacks during the time of the press releases.

root cause of the missing bitcoins until MtGox filed for bankruptcy.

Malleability attacks in period 2 and 3 could not contribute to the losses declared by MtGox since they happened after withdrawals have been stopped. Figure 6.2 visualizes both the number of bitcoins involved in malleability attacks as well as the number of attacks during period 1. During this period a total of 421 conflict sets were identified for a total value of 1,811.58 bitcoins involved in these attacks. In combination with the above mentioned success rate of malleability attacks we conclude that overall malleability attacks did not have any substantial influence in the loss of bitcoins incurred by MtGox.

During period 2, we gathered 1,062 conflict sets, totalling 5,470 bitcoins. A noticeable increase of attacks at 17:00 UTC on February 9, from 0.15 attacks per hour to 132 attacks per hour. While we do not have any information about the time the second press release has been published, the measured increase in attacks at 17:00 UTC and the date on the press release, hints at a time between 0:00 and 2:00 JST. The sudden increase suggests that immediately following the press release other attackers started imitating the attack, attempting to exploit the same weakness that had allegedly been used against MtGox.

After the second press release, in period 3, there is a sudden spike in activity. Between February 10 and 11 we identified 25,752 individual attacks totalling 286,076 bitcoins, two orders of magnitude larger than all attacks from period 1 combined. A second, smaller, wave of attacks starts after February 15, with a total of 9,193 bitcoins. The attacks have since calmed, returning to levels comparable to those observed in period 1, before the press releases. Figure 6.3 summarizes the situation plotting the cumulative value and number of malleability attacks in February 2014, i.e., from the end of period 1 to period 3.

The strong correlation between the press releases and the ensuing attacks attempting to exploit the same weakness is a strong indicator that the attacks were indeed triggered by the press releases.

Assuming MtGox had disabled withdrawals like they stated in the first press release, these attacks can not have been aimed at MtGox. The attacks therefore where either attempts to investigate transaction malleability or they were aimed at other businesses attempting to imitate the purveyed attack for personal gain. The sheer amount of bitcoins involved in malleability attacks would suggest that the latter motive was prevalent.

It remains questionable whether other services have been informed by MtGox in time to brace for the sudden increase in malleability attacks. Should this not be the case then the press release may have harmed other businesses by triggering imitators to attack them.

### 6.3.3   Beyond Our Data

In the previous subsections we presented an analysis of malleability attacks based on data we collected for over a year preceding the bankruptcy filing by MtGox. We have limited the analysis to the timespan we have first-hand data, starting January 2013. Clearly attacks may have happened even before our measurements started. However, in our opinion, it is unlikely that transaction malleability was exploited on a large scale be-

fore our measurements, and not during our measurements. After all, why would an attacker, having found such a lucrative
attack before 2013, suddenly stop exploiting it? It seems more
likely that an attacker would use this risk-free and successful
attack more often and with larger amounts of bitcoins!

While it is not possible to detect all malleability attacks
without participating in the network at the time they occur,
we can estimate the number of attacks preceding our measurements, just by reading the blockchain. By far the most
common modification during our measurements was the use of
non-minimal push opcodes, over 98% out of all attacks use this
modification. Successful attacks, i.e., those that were eventually confirmed, can be found by searching for this modification
in the set of all confirmed transactions. Given the success rate
and the number of successful attacks we can extrapolate the
number of attacks that were attempted before our measurements began.

By inspecting all confirmed transactions for signature scripts
that do not use minimal push opcodes we found a total of 48
transactions, involving a total of 33.92 bitcoins, before our measurements started, i.e., in the period 2009 – 2012. Assuming
that the success rate of 21.34% did not change significantly,
we can extrapolate a total of less than 160 bitcoins involved
in a few hundreds of attempted malleability attacks preceding
our measurements. This is equivalent to less than 10% of the
attacks identified during our measurements.

Besides the temporal restriction of our study, we also restricted ourselves to one specific attack, made possible by transaction malleability. Malleability attacks as defined in Section
6.1.2 require that both the original and the modified transaction
are broadcast in the Bitcoin network. This reflects the description of the attack in the MtGox press release of February 10,
2014 [66].

In addition to broadcasting the transactions in the network,
MtGox also published withdrawal transactions on their website. This may have resulted in a different attack, only partially covered by this work. MtGox sometimes created invalid

transactions with non-canonical signatures which would not be forwarded by newer Bitcoin clients. An attacker could retrieve the invalid transactions, correct the signatures and release the corrected transactions into the network.

We were able to collect these invalid transactions until October 2013, but not after that. The collected invalid transactions were considered when creating the conflict sets and figures in the analysis. It is however possible that some transactions did not even reach the Bitcoin network, and that some different type of attack might have played a role in MtGox' loss. We would like to stress that this paper does focus on malleability attacks only, as defined by MtGox and in this paper. Other types of attacks are outside the scope of this paper.

Finally, it is worth noting that the attacks described in this work could have been countered by adhering to basic best practices. Failed transactions should not be automatically retried, since a failure to confirm is indicative of other errors, as would have been the case with non-canonical signatures or malleability attacks. Should automatic retrial be desired, then the transaction issuer must ensure that the same inputs are reused. By doing so the issuer ensures that the funds are transferred at most once, even if an attacker may arbitrarily delay the transaction or exploit transaction malleability to render the original transaction unrecognizable.

## 6.4    Related Work

Transaction malleability has been known about since at least 2010, when it was first documented. It has however received very little attention so far as it was categorized as a low priority issue.

Andrychowicz et al. [7, 8] mention transaction malleability as a potential problem in contracts and two party computations based on Bitcoin transactions. These schemes can be used for example to implement a fair coin toss [12], auctions or decentralized voting. Their method to eliminate transaction malleability in their protocols resembles our construction of conflict sets, i.e., eliminating malleable parts of the transaction in the hash calculation. However, they limit their observations to advanced schemes for encoding contracts and two party computations.

A related class of doublespending attacks, which we shall refer to as classical doublespending, has received far more attention. In this class of attacks the transaction issuer creates two transactions to defraud the receiving party. Karame et al. [47] first studied the problem of arising from fast transactions, i.e., accepting non-confirmed transactions. Rosenfeld [78] showed that the success probability of a doublespending attack can be further increased if coupled with computational resources. Bamert et al. [14] later improved the security of accepting fast payments by observing how transactions are propagated in the network.

To the best of our knowledge this paper is the first publication describing transaction malleability and the resulting malleability attack in detail.

## 6.5  Conclusion

The transaction malleability problem is real and should be considered when implementing Bitcoin clients. However, while Mt-Gox claimed to have lost 850,000 bitcoins due to malleability attacks, we merely observed a total of 302,000 bitcoins ever being involved in malleability attacks. Of these, only 1,811 bitcoins were in attacks before MtGox stopped users from withdrawing bitcoins. Even more, 78.64% of these attacks were ineffective. As such, barely 386 bitcoins could have been stolen using malleability attacks from MtGox or from other businesses. Even if all of these attacks were targeted against MtGox, MtGox needs to explain the whereabouts of 849,600 bitcoins.

# 7

# Trustless Fiduciary Audits

One factor which has driven widespread adoption of Bitcoin is the emergence of Bitcoin exchanges: companies which allow trading bitcoins with fiat currency, such as Euros and US dollars. Bitcoin exchanges have helped the adoption of Bitcoin in two ways. Firstly, before the advent of Bitcoin exchanges, the only way to come by bitcoins was to *mine* them oneself or to informally trade bitcoins with other participants. Exchanges have opened the Bitcoin market to parties who might otherwise not have been able to participate. Secondly, exchanges publish their trade books which establishes an accepted exchange rate between fiat currencies and bitcoins. This in turn allowed vendors to value their goods and services in bitcoins in accordance to the market rates in fiat currency.

Although Bitcoin exchanges have had a positive contribution to the Bitcoin economy, they are not without risks. In

Moore and Christin's analysis of the risks involved with Bitcoin exchanges [63] they analyse 40 Bitcoin exchanges, at the time of publication 18 of the 40 exchanges had ceased operation. Of those 18, 5 exchanges did not reimburse customers on closure, 6 exchanges claim that they did and for the remaining 7 there is no data available. Most of the collapsed Bitcoin exchanges were not long-lived [63], with their closure either being immediate or over a relatively short period of time.

Since the publication of that analysis the most high-profile exchange closure took place: the bankruptcy and closure of the Mt. Gox Bitcoin exchange, in which 650,000 bitcoins belonging to customers of the exchange were lost or stolen. At the time, Mt. Gox claimed that a flaw in the Bitcoin protocol was to blame for the loss of its client's bitcoins, a claim which has since been refuted [31]. At the time of the event, Mt. Gox was one of the longest-running exchanges in the Bitcoin market with its cumulative number of transactions accounting for approximately 70% of all Bitcoin transactions.

Bitcoin transactions are irreversible by design. Once a user has transferred her bitcoins to another user there is no way that she will get them back without the cooperation of the recipient. There is little recourse for the customer of an exchange: Bitcoin is new ground for insurers, regulators, and law enforcement who do not yet have any established methods for dealing with Bitcoin related legal issues.

In an effort to calm customers fears, some exchanges have taken to periodically publishing data proving their solvency: an anonymised list of their customers account balances and a list of Bitcoin addresses owned by the exchange along with a signature that proves the ownership. If the balance of the bitcoins available on the addresses is at least as large as the sum of the amounts owed by the exchange, the exchange is solvent. Although customers may be appreciative of this type of transparency, it may put the exchange at a disadvantage as it reveals information of strategic importance, such as the number of customers, the amounts the exchange's customers keep on hand and the total balance of bitcoins held by the exchange.

In conventional financial markets trust is placed in the financial statements made by institutions such as exchanges or investment funds through the process of auditing. An independent third party, which is perceived to be trustworthy by the customers of the institution, or a state mandated auditor inspects the financial records of the institution and publishes an audit result. Such an audit is an expensive and time-consuming process and is typically only performed in well-spaced intervals.

In this chapter, we proposed to perform a software-based audit of Bitcoin exchanges without revealing any information about the bitcoins that are possessed by either the exchange, or its customers to the public. This is achieved by replacing the human financial auditor by a piece of software. To ensure that the software is executed correctly we rely on Trusted Computing (TC) technology. In our scenario, the traditional limitations of financial auditing no longer apply. Software executes orders of magnitudes faster than humans, and the execution of a piece of software is generally not costly at all and it becomes feasible to provide daily audits of a Bitcoin exchange. Our contribution is twofold: we propose a system that uses Trusted Computing to prove the exchange's solvibility to its customers and we implement the proposed solution on consumer hardware minimizing obstacles to its deployment.

### 7.0.1 Related Work

Auditing Bitcoin exchanges was first discussed by Maxwell and Todd [54], and later by Maxwell and Wilcox [55]. Both approaches rely on modifying the merkle tree computation to defend against insertion of negative subtrees. Our use of TC for the merkle tree computation obviates any such modifications as the secure code would error out on negative sums.

Trusted Computing, and more specifically TPMs, have been proposed previously as a method to secure Bitcoin wallets by Hal Finney [37], storing sensitive keying material in the tamper proof storage. Since then several additional methods of securing funds have been proposed, including multisignature accounts [5], the creation of deterministic public keys that do not require private keys during the generation [9] and locking funds for a predetermined period of time [83]. The latter may also be used to extend the audit to guarantee the solvency for a certain period, by making the funds inccessible until they are unlocked.

While regular audits may help detect fraud at an early stage, a regulatory framework is needed to prosecute perpetrators. Some initial work has been done in the field of regulation, examining the impact of Bitcoin on current anti-money laundering (AML) policies and on know-your-customer (KYC) policies [1, 3, 20, 22, 70].

## 7.1    Preliminaries

The software-based audit of a Bitcoin exchange relies on an understanding of both the Bitcoin project as well as Trusted Computing. This section introduces the fundamentals of Bitcoin and Trusted Computing, as needed in this paper.

### 7.1.1    Bitcoin

Bitcoin is a decentralized digital currency built on cryptographic protocols and a system of *proof of work*. Instead of relying on traditional, centralized financial institutions to administer transactions as well as other aspects concerning the economic valuation of the currency, peers within the Bitcoin network process transactions and control the creation of bitcoins. The major problems to be solved by a distributed currency are related to how consensus can be reached in a group of anonymous participants, some of whom may be behaving with malicious intent.

Transactions within the Bitcoin network are based on public key cryptography, users of Bitcoin generate an *address* which is used to receive funds. The Bitcoin address is derived, through cryptographic hash functions, from the public-key of an ECDSA key pair. A Bitcoin transaction records the transfer of bitcoins from some input address to output addresses. A transaction consists of one or more inputs and one or more outputs, each input to a transaction is the output of a previous transaction. The output of a transaction may only be used as the input to a single transaction. The outputs are associated with an address, whose private key is then used to sign transactions spending these outputs.

Transactions are generated by the sender and distributed amongst the peers in the Bitcoin network. Transactions are only valid once they have been accepted into the public history of transactions, the *blockchain*. As the blockchain contains Bitcoin's entire transaction history and is publicly distributed, any user can determine the bitcoin balance of every address at any time, by summing the value of unspent transaction outputs (UTXOs) associated with the address.

**Bitcoin Exchanges**

Bitcoin exchanges facilitate trade between fiat currency and bitcoins. In order to trade on the exchange, users create an account with the exchange and transfer fiat currency and/or bitcoins to the exchange. Should the user wish to retrieve their bitcoins, they must make a request that the exchange transfers the bitcoins to an address which the user controls. The exchange manages a balance of the bitcoins that the user has deposited with the exchange or traded for against fiat currency.

The user may place buy and sell orders for bitcoins or fiat currency which are executed for the user by the exchange, adjusting the balances of the user's Bitcoin or fiat currency accounts. The orders are executed internally within the exchange, that is they are not recorded in the blockchain. Given this model of operation, a Bitcoin exchange is not merely a marketplace but also acts as a fiduciary, administrating both fiat currency and bitcoin accounts for its clients.

## 7.1.2   Trusted Computing

When a third party, such as a Bitcoin exchange, is tasked with performing a computation, there is no method for the verification of the integrity of the result, short of performing the computation locally, which in some circumstances may not be feasible. Trusted Computing allows the creation of a *trusted platform* which provides the following features [84]:

**Protected Capabilities**   are commands which may access *shielded locations*, areas in memory or registers which are only accessible to the trusted platform. These memory areas may contain sensitive data such as private keys or a digest of some aspect of the current system state.

**Integrity Measurement** is the process of *measuring* the software which is executing on the current platform. A measurement is the cryptographic hash of the software which is executing throughout each stage of execution.

**Integrity Reporting** is the process of delivering a platform measurement to a third party such that it can be verified to have originated from a trusted platform.

These features of the trusted platform are deployed on consumer hardware in a unit called the Trusted Platform Module (TPM), a secure cryptographic co-processor, which is usually incorporated on the mainboard of the hardware.

An important component in proving trust are the Platform Configuration Registers (PCRs), 20-byte registers which are only modifiable through the *extend* operation based on cryptographic hash digests. The properties of a cryptographic hash ensure that the value held in a PCR cannot be deliberately set.

Initially the TPM is equipped with a Storage Root Key (SRK) which may be used to sign and thus authenticate further keys which may be generated or loaded into the TPM. A number of different types of cryptographic keys may be present on the TPM, however we limit our description to Attestation Identity Keys (AIK). AIKs are signing keys that reside solely on the TPM, which are used to sign data, which originates from the TPM, in order to attest to the values originating from the TPM. In order to verify a TPM attestation, the verifying party requires the signed attestation, the AIK public key, and a valid SRK signature authenticating the AIK.

The TPM can be used to *seal* data which encrypts the data with a key which is loaded in the TPM and binds the data to the state of some of the PCRs. The encrypted data may only be decrypted or *unsealed* if PCRs are in the same state as when the data was sealed, thus binding the ability to decrypt to the measured state. TPMs provide two distinct paradigms:

**SRTM** (Static Root of Trust for Measurement): the system begins to boot in a piece of firmware which is trusted (the static root) and each component of the boot process is measured and verified against a known-good configuration before it is executed in order to assert that no component has been tampered with.

**DRTM** (Dynamic Root of Trust for Measurement): allows for a trusted platform to be established dynamically without requiring a system reboot. It even allows for a trusted platform to be established within a platform which is known to be compromised with malicious software.

DRTM is implemented in consumer general purpose processors from Intel and AMD under the names Intel Trusted eXecution Technology (TXT) and AMD Secure Virtual Machine (SVM). Intel TXT and AMD SVM provide additional security features when executing in the secure mode on top of the capabilities of the TPM. These include turning off system interrupts to prevent other execution paths, as well as memory protection for specific memory ranges which also prevents DMA access [43].

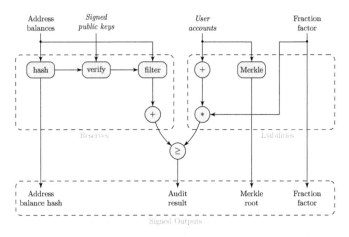

**Figure 7.1:** An overview of the audit process. Italicised values are not published.

## 7.2   Auditing

The audit should determine the solvency of the exchange. In principle this is a binary result, either *solvent* in the case that the exchange's assets in bitcoins cover its liabilities in bitcoins, or *insolvent* otherwise. It is plausible that there are situations in which this binary result does not suffice, for instance an exchange which wishes to prove fractional reserves. In these cases a multiplicative factor can be applied to the liabilities of the exchange to show that the exchange can cover some percentage of its liabilities with its assets.

The auditing process can be broken into three individual steps: summing the user account balances (proof of liabilities), summing the assets, i.e., address balances, the exchange controls (proof of reserves), and proof that the reserves cover the liabilities (proof of solvency). Figure 7.1 illustrates the components of the audit, the inputs to each of the components of the calculation and the outputs of the audit.

The publicly available inputs are the address balance and the fraction factor, which determines the percentage of coverage that the exchange wishes to prove. The address balances can be computed by a third party by replaying transactions in the blockchain until the time of the audit. The non-public inputs consist of a list of signed public keys owned by the exchange and the list of user account information, including account balances and customer identifiers.

Unlike the inputs, the outputs of the auditing process should all be disclosed publicly. The address balance hash proves that the latest snapshot of the address balances was used in the audit and should match an independently computed hash. The audit result is the boolean result, either `true` if the exchanges assets are greater than the fraction of the liabilities or `false` otherwise. To prove that all liabilities have been considered a merkle tree is computed and its root is included in the outputs as well as the fraction which determines the coverage percentage. The output values are signed by the TPM, which also signs a hash digest of the binary which was executing at the time.

## 7.2.1 Proof of Reserves

The assets that the exchange possesses are in the form of bitcoins in the blockchain. The sum of assets is therefore calculated by determining which balances in the blockchain the exchange has access to and calculating the sum of those balances. In order for the exchange to access the bitcoins it needs to be in possession of the private keys belonging to the addresses.

To simplify the calculation, the audit program does not need to parse the entire blockchain to determine which balances should be summed. Instead, a preprocessor can be used to compute the address balances from the blockchain. This is secure as it is a deterministic aggregation over publicly available data.

The exchange can prove control of a Bitcoin address by providing the public key belonging to that Bitcoin address and signing it with the private key. For additional safety, the exchange should also sign a value which can be used to prove the freshness of the signature, a nonce. The hash of the last block added to the blockchain is an ideal candidate for the nonce, as it uniquely identifies the state of the blockchain and thus the address balances, it is not predictable and changes frequently. Thus, the second input to the audit process consists of a list of tuples of a public keys, and a signatures of the public key and the nonce:

$$\langle \text{PubKey}, \{\text{PubKey}, \text{Nonce}\}_\sigma \rangle$$

where $\{\text{data}\}_\sigma$ indicates that *data* is signed with the corresponding private key.

The overview of the steps of the calculation of reserves is shown in Figure 7.1, internally it consists of four different stages. The first stage computes the hash of the address balances, which is required in the *verify* stage. The verify stage asserts that the signatures for the public keys are valid and that the provided nonce matches the hash of the provided address balances. It then passes the public keys to the *filter* stage, determines the Bitcoin address and filters for entries in the address balances which match the exchange's addresses. Finally, the balances of these entries are summed. The sum, as well as the hash of the address balances are produced as outputs of the proof of reserves.

## 7.2.2   Proof of Liabilities

The liabilities of the exchange are the balances in bitcoins owed to its customers. The audit process requires a list of tuples consisting of a customer identifier and a positive balance owed to the customer:

$$\langle \text{CustID}, \text{Balance} \rangle$$

An additional input to the proof of liabilities is the *fraction factor*, which is multiplied with the sum of client account balances to prove fractional reserves.

Using the above definition of liabilities, the total liabilities of the exchange are calculated as the sum of all customer account balances. The calculated sum is later compared against the sum of reserves to determine solvency. Additionally to the sum, the proof of liabilities component calculates the root of a merkle tree [57], as well as a hash of the fraction factor.

The basic schema is to construct a merkle tree with the user account information. That is, in order to compute a leaf in the tree one would take the cryptographic hash of the customer identifier and the balance owed to the customer. The leaves are then combined in a pairwise fashion and hashed, forming the nodes in the next layer of the tree. Nodes are combined and hashed until the root of the tree is constructed.

As the root of the merkle tree is dependent on all of the individual values within the tree, it serves as public record of the account balances which were counted in the summation of all account balances, without revealing individual customers account balances.

### 7.2.3 Proof of Solvency and Verification

The proof of the solvency of a bitcoin exchange consists of two components, one is the outputs of the audit, the other is an attestation which can be used to verify that the auditing software was executed in the trusted environment, and that it computed the outputs which are attested. The final output is the *Audit result*, which is a binary value, *true* if the reserves are greater than or equal to the liabilities, and *false* otherwise. The attestation is a signature for the outputs as well as the platform measurements, i.e., the hashes of the executed program.

Given the audit program, its public inputs and outputs and the attestation, a customer can independently verify the validity of the audit. By hashing the program and validating it against the attested measurements she can ensure that the TPM has executed the program. The validity of the program could be proven by publishing its source code. The customer can then proceed to validating the outputs, by checking the sig-

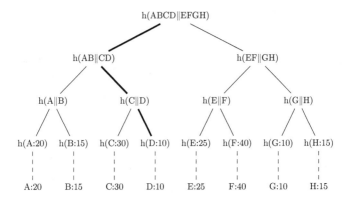

**Figure 7.2:** An example merkle tree with the path from h(D:10) to the root highlighted

natures, that the address balance hash matches the blockchain and that she is included in the merkle tree.

The customer can use the root of the merkle tree to verify that its account balance was included in the calculation. The merkle tree in Figure 7.2 shows a potential scenario in which customer D wishes to determine whether it was accounted for in the hash h(ABCD‖EFGH). The nodes which D requires are the children of the nodes along the path from D's leaf node to the root excluding the nodes along that path. These are the nodes h(C:30), $h(A \parallel B)$, h(EF‖GH). With these node values, D can reconstruct the path from its leaf node to the root, calculating the same value of h(ABCD‖EFGH) that was provided by the exchange.

## 7.3    Implementation

The proof-of-concept presented in this work is built on the Flicker platform [56]. Flicker is a software platform which leverages DRTM to allow security sensitive components of software applications to execute in a secure, isolated environment. The developers of Flicker call such a component a Piece of Application Logic (PAL). The PAL comprises only the routines required to perform some security critical computation component of the application. Flicker consists of two components, the kernel module which prepares and launches the DRTM process, and the Secure Loader Block (SLB) core which performs bootstrapping of the secure execution environment for the PAL.

The execution scenario in which the PAL runs is made up of four distinct components: the user application, the Flicker kernel module, an Authenticated Code Module (ACM), and one or more PAL binaries, each consisting of the SLB core and PAL. The ACM is the root of dynamic trust for the DRTM in Intel TXT and is digitally signed by the chipset vendor. It functions as a secure bootloader for a lightweight piece of code which is to be executed on the processor in complete isolation from any other software or hardware access.

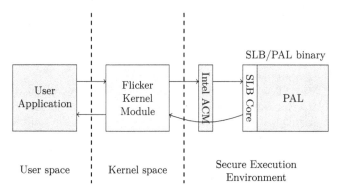

**Figure 7.3:** Flicker PAL execution scenario.

The user application is a conventional application executing in userspace. The Flicker kernel module provides **data** and **control** file system entries with which the user application may interact in order to provide the Flicker kernel module with the SLB, PAL, and the inputs, as well as to read the outputs when execution of the PAL terminates.

Figure 7.3 illustrates the control flow when the user application needs to perform a security-critical task. First the application passes the PAL binary and inputs to the Flicker kernel module and instructs the kernel module to execute the PAL. The Flicker kernel module prepares the necessary data structures and memory protection to launch the DRTM and start the PAL, it then invokes the GETSEC[SENTER] CPU instruction which disables interrupts and triggers the start of the DRTM. These data structures are measured by the Intel ACM, which forms the root of the DRTM. The ACM hands control over to the Flicker SLB core which invokes the PAL and contains the necessary data structures to return the control flow directly to the Flicker kernel module when the PAL has finished executing.

During the execution of the SENTER operation, the dynamic TPM PCRs (17-23) are initialised to zero. PCR 17 is then extended with the hashes of the ACM and a number of configuration parameters. During the execution, PCR 18 is extended with the hash of the PAL. These PCR values are provided in the TPM's attestation, which can be used to prove to a third party that the PAL binary was executed and calculated the output values.

The Flicker platform was designed with lightweight, short-lived computations in mind, as such it imposes a number of restrictions which make a direct implementation of the audit as outlined in Chapter 7.2 unfeasible. The major restriction which poses problems for the automated software audit is memory. The Flicker environment has a stack size of 4KB, a heap size of 128KB, and a maximum input size of approximately 116KB. In addition each Flicker session has a significant overhead, between 0.2 and 1 second, depending on which TPM functionality is used during the invocation [56].

## 7.3.1   Architecture

Three of the four inputs to the audit process may be of considerable size: the address balances, the public keys and signatures, and the user accounts. At the time of writing there are a total of 3.7 million addresses with a non-zero balance. Each of the entries in the address balance input consists of an address of up to 35 byte and a 64 bit integer for the balance. The size of all address balances therefore is just under 160 MB. The size of the user accounts depends on the number of user accounts of the exchange. Generating a unique identifier from the account information by hashing results in a 32 byte identifier. Each account therefore has a 32 byte identifier with a 64 bit integer for the balance. Estimating the user base of the exchange at 1 million users this results in a total size for the user account input of 40 MB. While the number of addresses owned by the exchange is under control of the exchange, the prototype should support any number of addresses.

It is clear from the memory requirements posed by the input data and the available input sizes of the Flicker platform that the monolithic architecture of the audit as proposed in Figure 7.1 must be broken into smaller components. The input data is split into input-sized chunks and processed in an incremental fashion. This does not change the result of the audit, however the calculation of the outputs which are required to verify the input data must change as a result of the components only having a view of a small subset of the input data in each iteration. The individual invocations of a component of the audit require a secure method of storing intermediate values, for instance a sum which is calculated over multiple iterations. The PAL can use the TPM to seal intermediate values to the current PCR state, encrypting them such that they can only be decrypted by the TPM when it is executing the same PAL. The encrypted data is passed back to the user application which should provide it as an input to the next iteration of the component.

The process is driven by a user application, external to the trusted platform, which repeatedly invokes the computation in the trusted platform. As the encrypted data is passed back to the user application, which is executing in an untrusted and potentially malicious environment, there is the potential for a

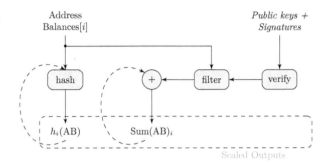

**Figure 7.4:** An overview of the proof of reserves component. Italicised values are not published publicly. Dashed arrows indicate values which are passed from invocation to invocation

replay attack to be performed. However, the process of hashing the input ensures that replay attacks can be detected by the client when verifying the result of the audit.

We consider each component of the system individually and describe how it is implemented in order to support incremental invocations.

**Proof of Reserves**   The Proof of Reserves can be split into iterative invocations by splitting the address balance list, and the list of signatures and public keys into equal sized batches. Initially the address balance list is sorted lexicographically, in order to allow a verifier to compute the same hash. Each batch contains a list of address balances and a possibly empty set of signatures and public keys matching the address balances of the batch. This allows the system to verify the signatures and sum up the respective values. The hash of the address balances is computed by concatenating the hash from the previous round with the current hash and hashing the result: $h_0 = h(AB_0)$ and $h_i = h(h_{i-1} \parallel AB_i)$. The output includes the last considered address from the current batch. Due to the lexicographic ordering of addresses it is trivial for the proof of reserves to detect a replay attack, since it would require a lexicographically lower first address than the last address from the previous batch. Figure 7.4 shows an overview of the new POR component.

**Proof of Liabilities** The Proof of Liabilities (POL) is invoked iteratively, similarly to the Proof of Reserves. Figure 7.5 shows an overview of the POL component. The merkle tree computation accepts a list of tuples consisting of merkle subtree root hashes, the root's height and the associated sum of the tree's value. It then iteratively computes the roots of the trees by combining the subtrees, summing the values and increasing the height. The resulting merkle root, height and value sum is then sealed for the next iteration or to be passed to the proof of solvency. In order to initiate the process, the proof of liabilities also accepts subtrees that are not sealed for height 0, i.e., the hashes of the account identifier and the account's value. Missing branches in the merkle tree are replaced with a single leaf with value 0.

Given that the merkle tree computation does not allow negative value sums for subtrees guarantees that, if an account was included in the computation, its value is included in the sum. A replay attack in this case does not benefit the exchange as it may only increase the sum that is to be covered.

**Proof of Solvency** The Proof of Solvency (POS) component takes as inputs the sealed outputs from the Proof of Reserves (POR) and Proof of Liabilities (POS) components as well as the Fraction factor. As it handles only constant size inputs it is sufficient to call the proof of solvability once. Its main purpose is to compute the fraction that is to be covered and whether or not the assets are sufficient to cover the liabilities. A secondary purpose is to unseal the results from the other components and sign in order to publish them.

The final step of the POS component is the attestation of the PAL binary. The audit no longer consists of an individual

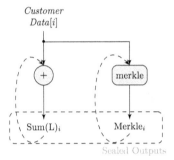

**Figure 7.5:** An overview of the proof of liabilities component. Italicised values are not published publicly. Dashed arrows indicate values which are passed from invocation to invocation

invocation of a PAL, instead the POR and POL components are invoked hundreds or thousands of times each of these invocations requires attestation. The solution to this problem is to put the separate logic for the POR, POL and POS components into a single binary. The initial invocations of both the POR and POL logic of the PAL produce a sealed intermediate values which are tied to that PAL. The sealed blob is then unsealed by the next invocation, the intermediate values are modified and then resealed. When the POS is invoked, it unseals the intermediate results produced by the POR and POL.

The fact that the sealed blobs are unsealed and modified in each invocation of the POR and POL and that they can only be unsealed by the same PAL that initially created them means that the values in the sealed blob form a chain of trust from their respective first invocations until the invocation of the POS. An attesation of the POS is transitive to all previous PAL executions which were able to unseal the blobs that the POS unseals.

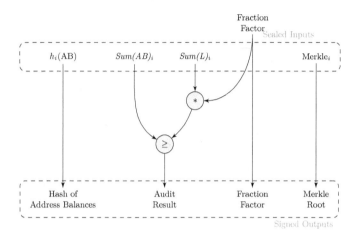

**Figure 7.6:** An overview of the proof of solvency component.

## 7.3.2 Execution time

As previously mentioned, the Flicker invocation and some TPM operations pose a significant overhead of up to $1s$, when repeatedly entering and leaving the PAL. During the execution time of the PAL, the operating system on which the Flicker session is invoked does not process any interrupts. When the Flicker session ends, the operating system requires a small amount of time to process any interrupts and respond to system events. Tests showed that the operating system needs pauses of $500ms$ to $1s$ in order to continue processing without locking up or crashing. As the processing time for such a small number of inputs is quite low in comparison to the TPM overhead, we can safely assume that each Flicker invocation costs approximately two seconds.

For input sizes in the range previously discussed, 3.7 million address balances and 1 million customer accounts, the POR must be invoked approximately 1300 times if each invocation of the POR can process 3000 address balances, the POL must be invoked approximately 500 times. This comes to a total of 1800 invocations, each of which requires 2s to execute and wait for the operating system to recover. The overall execution time for an audit with inputs of this size is approximately one hour and scales linearly in the number of address balances and user accounts.

### 7.3.3   Additional Interfaces

Although the audit is the core component of proving solvency of a Bitcoin exchange, the signed audit output is not all that a customer requires in order to verify the audit. Customers must retrieve additional values from the exchange and perform some local computations in order to be able to verify the audit, and to have some form of recourse should the verification fail. The implementation of these interfaces is not in the scope of this work, what follows is an outline of the requirements of the peripheral software and interfaces.

#### Audit Verification

Most important for customers is the ability to verify the audit's result. This consists of the verification that the customer's balance was included in the calculation, verification of the address balances, and verification of the attestation. The customer of an exchange must be able to retrieve the nodes in the merkle tree which can be used to calculate the path from the customer's leaf node to the root of the merkle tree. If the customer is able to reproduce the merkle root using the nodes provided by the exchange and their own customer identifier and account balance at the time of the audit, then they can be assured that they were accounted for in the calculation. The interface for this purpose must take the hash of the tuple

$$\langle \text{Customer Identifier}, \text{Balance} \rangle$$

as an argument and deliver the set of nodes required to calculate the path from the customer's leaf node to the merkle root. Each node would consist of a tuple

$$\langle Height, Hash \rangle$$

Where *Height* is the height of the node in the merkle tree and *Hash* is the hash digest stored at that node in the tree. The customer must also be able to verify that the hash of the address balances provided by the exchange represents the true account balances for a set blockchain height. For this purpose, the customer must be able to determine the blockchain height that was used to determine the address balances. The customer would require a software client which can determine the address balances for the blockchain at a given height. This consists of: extraction and aggregation of UTXOs, and sorting of the address balances. With the address balances calculated, the customer can calculate the hash and compare it with the hash provided by the audit. Finally, the customer must be able to verify the attestation. This consists of two components: verification that the attestation originates from a TPM, and verification of the binary which was executed in the trusted platform.

**Attestation Verification** The customer needs to be able to verify that the attestation was indeed issued by a TPM, in other words, what the customer needs to know is that the Attestation Identity Key (AIK) used to sign the attestion was provided by a TPM. The method proposed by the TCG is Direct Anonymous Attestation (DAA) which allows for a customer to verify directly that an AIK belongs to a TPM. For this the exchange must provide an interface which performs DAA and the customer requires client software which can verify the DAA provided by the exchange.

**Binary Verification** In order for the customer to verify that the PAL executed in the trusted environment actually calculates the audit, as opposed to always returning true, the customer must have access to the source code of the PAL and be able to reproduce the value of PCR 17 which is signed in the TPM's attestation. The exchange needs to provide a platform from which the PAL source code can be retrieved, as well as a method for compiling a reproducible binary, and instructions on how to transform the hash of the binary to the value of PCR 17 in the attestation.

**Signed Account Balance**

If a customer should determine that their account balance was not included in an audit, they require some form of proof that their account balances ought to have been taken into account in the audit. For this purpose the exchange should provide an interface which allows a customer to retrieve a signature of the hash of their $\langle CustomrID, balance \rangle$ tuple. With this signature, other customers or the community at large could verify that the exchange signed a value which is not included in the latest audit.

## 7.4    Conclusion

A string of Bitcoin exchange closures as well as various thefts from Bitcoin exchanges have left customers of exchange services somewhat hesitant as there has often been little transparency when such events took place. Exchanges have published customer account balances as well as proof of ownership of Bitcoin addressed which allow for customers and the public to determine the Bitcoin assets of the exchange.

In this work we propose using an automated software-based audit to determine the solvency of Bitcoin exchanges without revealing any private data. Methods are proposed, based on the Flicker Trusted Computing platform, with which the audit result can be verified and trusted to be correct. An architecture is proposed which allows for the computation to be split into individual pieces which iteratively compute a subset of the complete input to overcome the memory limitations posed by the Flicker platform. The verification methodology is expanded to cover the iterative execution scenario, allowing for customers of an exchange to verify the inputs to the audit. An analysis of the execution time showed that it is entirely feasible to conduct audits on a daily basis at the current estimate size of the Bitcoin ecosystem.

# 8

# Securing Fast Payments

Today, we are witnessing that an increasing number of payments in our economy are executed digitally and cashlessly. Entire businesses are founded upon e-commerce and established companies are looking for new ways to expand their existing payment methods. In the last years, several new payment systems like Google Wallet or PayPal simplified fast and mobile money exchange. These approaches have in common that they rely on a central trusted authority to process payments. In contrast, the Bitcoin currency and payment system offers a completely decentralized payment infrastructure based on a peer-to-peer network. Even though there is no central trust authority, the Bitcoin network can provide reliable international money transfer.

However, due to the decentralized nature of Bitcoin, transactions can only be confirmed if the majority of participat-

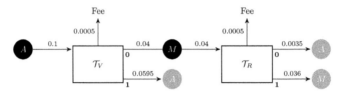

**Figure 8.1:** Transaction chain for the return transaction $\mathcal{T}_R$ in the case of too many funds sent by the attacker. The attacker's wallet address is denoted by $A$, the current merchant's wallet address by $M$. The price of the good is 0.036 bitcoins and this amount would be effectively claimed by the merchant. The rest is returned to the attacker with fees deducted.

ing nodes accepts them. This transaction confirmation process can take several minutes. Although often touted as the digital equivalent of cash it is not fit for interactions that require fast clearing of transactions. While this delay is not problematic for most online purchases, it prevents the use of Bitcoin in situations where a transaction confirmation is required in the order of seconds, such as paying in a supermarket or at a snack vending machine.

In this chapter, we present a concept that improves the trade-off between transaction speed and confirmation reliability in the Bitcoin network. In addition to our double-spending experiments that quantify this trade-off, we implemented the fast transaction mechanism in a common snack vending machine that now accepts bitcoins as a payment and dispenses the product within seconds.

## 8.1   Bitcoin

Bitcoin was introduced as a peer-to-peer digital currency in 2008 by Satoshi Nakamoto [68]. Traditionally, cashless transactions between two entities require an issuing/clearing authority which will act as a trusted third party. In Bitcoin, the entire computer network fulfills the role of the trusted third party for transactions between accounts, where nodes in the network propagate and verify transactions. The nodes implement a replicated ledger that keeps track of the account balances, verifies transactions against its current state and updates account balances accordingly. In contrast to other cashless payment systems, Bitcoin transactions are irreversible once they have been accepted by the network. As a consequence, Bitcoin has comparatively low transaction fees and no charge-backs, the downside being that money lost through theft or fraud is non-refundable.

A transaction in the Bitcoin network describes the transfer of a specific amount of bitcoins from one account to another. Transactions are represented as signed data structures that are broadcast into the Bitcoin network and recorded by the nodes. It is comprised of references to one or more previous transactions that funded the spending party and an assignment of a specific amount of bitcoins to one or more addresses. A transaction is atomic in the sense that the claiming of bitcoins from the previous transactions is inseparably linked to the transfer of these bitcoins to the receiving account. The references to previous transactions are referred to as *inputs* to the transaction, whereas the account and the amount of bitcoins that it ought to receive are called *outputs*. After the transfer, the owner of the receiving account has new funds at her disposal to spend in future transactions. The balance of an account is the sum of the values of all unspent outputs owned by that account.

It is important to note that as soon as an output is claimed and used as an input to a transaction it may not be reused. This means that a single output may not be used as an input to multiple transactions. The violation of this principle is referred to as *double-spending*.

When a user wants to transfer bitcoins to another user, she creates a transaction specifying outputs as well as inputs and signs the transaction. The transaction is then broadcast through the network using a flood broadcast. Each node verifies that (a) the output value of the transaction does not exceed the input value, (b) outputs are spent only once and (c) that the signatures match the sending account. If the transaction passes validation, the nodes will forward it to their neighbors.

Eventually, the network will confirm the transaction by including it into the public ledger. The transaction confirmation is a crucial step but also the most time-consuming. In expectation, it takes 10 minutes for the network to reach consensus about a set of transactions. A confirmation time in the order of minutes is undesirable for use-cases where purchased products are expected to be released to the customer immediately. However, merchants may choose not to wait for the confirmation of incoming transactions and release products as soon as they notice the transactions in the network. This is called a *fast payment*.

Fast payments build upon trusting a transaction to be eventually confirmed. It is a common suggestion by the Bitcoin community that the trade-off of not waiting for the definitive transaction confirmation should be accepted for low-priced goods where instant delivery is desired and possible loss of revenue marginal.

## 8.2 Related Work

Double-spends and fast payments were first analyzed by Karame et al. [47]. They found that double-spend attempts have a non-negligible probability of success. We expand on their result by considering a merchant that has a random sample of connected nodes in the network and does not accept incoming connections. Furthermore, we avoid isolating the merchant by not forwarding transactions destined for it and describe a method to securely return overpaid or incomplete payments.

The public ledger that tracks transactions in the Bitcoin network might be interesting for merchants as it would allow the creation of customer profiles. However, the initial publication by Nakamoto [68] claimed that transactions in the Bitcoin network are pseudonymous, which would make binding an account to its owner difficult. A first analysis of the anonymity was done by Reid and Harrigan [73], which used information from the publicly available ledger to connect multiple addresses to relinquish information about their owner. Ron and Shamir [75], among other things, attempted to infer patterns from individual transactions. ZeroCoin [58], a system that uses zero-knowledge proofs as a claiming condition of transactions, would allow truly anonymous transactions in which bitcoins can be acquired without a direct connection between sender and receiver.

With the recently published reports of the European Central Bank [2], the US department of treasury [3] and the FBI [1], Bitcoin received the needed legal status that allows its adoption at a large scale. Widespread adoption is a major requirement for merchants to begin using Bitcoin as a payment alternative. These reports were preceded by a first analysis of the legality of Bitcoin by Elias [35] in 2011.

## 8.3 Securing Fast Payments

A merchant accepting fast payments incurs the risk of acting on a transaction that will not be confirmed by the network. This might result in a financial loss for the merchant.

An attacker attempting to defraud the merchant may try to double-spend the payment in order to receive the good or service from the merchant without paying for it. We assume that the attacker may connect to an arbitrary number of nodes in the network and broadcast any number of transactions claiming outputs in its possession. However, the attacker may not inhibit the communication between nodes and may not identify the neighbors of a node. To perform a double-spending attack, the attacker would create two transactions $\mathcal{T}_A$ and $\mathcal{T}_V$. Both transactions spend the same output and can therefore not both be valid. $\mathcal{T}_V$ denotes the transaction that transfers the required amount to the merchant, whereas $\mathcal{T}_A$ is a transaction that transfers the same amount back to the attacker. The attacker then attempts to convince the merchant about the validity of $\mathcal{T}_V$, while broadcasting $\mathcal{T}_A$ to the network at the same time. For the double-spending attempt to succeed two conditions have to be met: (a) the merchant should only see $\mathcal{T}_V$ until the good or service is released, and (b) $\mathcal{T}_A$ must be confirmed by the Bitcoin network, hence $\mathcal{T}_V$ would not be valid.

The risk for the merchant is further amplified by *information eclipsing* [30]. If the merchant forwards $\mathcal{T}_V$ to its neighboring nodes, they will verify and tentatively commit it to the local ledger. Should they later receive $\mathcal{T}_A$, it will not be considered valid as it conflicts with $\mathcal{T}_V$, and it will not be forwarded to the merchant. The merchant inadvertently shields itself against conflicting transactions like $\mathcal{T}_A$, and will be unaware of the double-spending attempt.

### 8.3.1   Countermeasures

To harden against the aforementioned attack, we propose several countermeasures. First and foremost, it has to be guaranteed that the attacker is not the only source of information. To this end, the merchant should connect to a sufficiently large random sample of nodes in the Bitcoin network. By doing so, the attacker cannot inject faulty transaction information to reach the merchant, because she does not know over which nodes the merchant communicates.

Secondly, the merchant should not accept incoming connections. Thus an attacker cannot directly send $\mathcal{T}_V$ to the merchant. Forcing the attacker to broadcast it over the network will ensure that $\mathcal{T}_V$ ends up in the local view of those nodes that forward it. Subsequent transactions using the same inputs, e.g. $\mathcal{T}_A$, would be duly ignored by those nodes, alleviating the risk that $\mathcal{T}_A$ ends up in the public ledger.

Furthermore, the merchant can effectively avoid isolation by not relaying transaction $\mathcal{T}_V$. This way, the attacker would have to shield all of the merchant's connected nodes from $\mathcal{T}_A$ in order to keep the merchant isolated. As soon as a single node is uninfluenced by the attacker, it will forward $\mathcal{T}_A$ to the merchant, thus informing the merchant of the attempted double-spend. In addition, by not relaying transactions, the merchant protects itself against timing attacks. An attacker could otherwise monitor and time relayed transactions in order to map out the merchant's connected nodes. The remainder of the network will ensure that the transaction is propagated to all nodes, hence not relaying the transaction has only a negligible effect on its propagation.

The merchant examines the *propagation depth* of $\mathcal{T}_V$, i.e., a listening period before the transaction is accepted by the merchant. Throughout this period, it would be imprudent of the attacker to attempt the double-spend, as any of the merchant's connected nodes could detect it. After the listening period, the legitimate transaction $\mathcal{T}_V$ will have propagated through a sufficiently large part of the network. If the attacker were to broadcast $\mathcal{T}_A$, only a minority of nodes in the network would forward it, thus drastically reducing the probability that $\mathcal{T}_A$ is ever included in the public ledger.

## 8.3.2 Return Chaining

The merchant needs a mechanism to return money to the customer. We can distinguish three possible transaction scenarios in which money is returned. Firstly, a transaction can be underspent and the insufficient funds are returned. Secondly, a transaction can be overspent, in which case the customer is entitled to change. Lastly, the customer could cancel the transaction, which would also make her entitled to the amount of money she already provided to the merchant.

In the presence of double-spending attacks, it is not only important how many bitcoins have to be returned, but also where they originated from. The merchant may simply create a transaction $\mathcal{T}_R$ from its account, that sends the amount to return to the customer's account. This transaction, however, would be valid independently from whether the customer's transaction $\mathcal{T}_V$ is valid or not. An attacker could attempt a double-spending attack and trigger a return payment. In case of an unsuccessful attack, the attacker would receive the return without losing anything. If the attack is successful, the attacker would receive the double-spent amount plus the return payment.

In order to avoid being vulnerable to this type of attack, the merchant has to ensure that if $\mathcal{T}_V$ is not valid, then also $\mathcal{T}_R$ is not valid as well. This automatic invalidation of the return transaction is possible by using a mechanism called *return chaining*. Return chaining means that the merchant claims the output created as a result of $\mathcal{T}_V$ and uses it as an input to $\mathcal{T}_R$ (cfr. Figure 8.1). This enables the merchant to immediately return change without the need of a confirmation. Should the attacker succeed in double-spending $\mathcal{T}_V$, the network would eventually reach consensus that $\mathcal{T}_V$ is not valid, the outputs would not be created and thus could not be claimed by any transaction. As $\mathcal{T}_R$ is a transaction claiming one of the outputs of $\mathcal{T}_V$ it would automatically be invalid.

## 8.4　Evaluation

To evaluate the accuracy of the proposed system to detect and reject double-spends we implemented the attacker and the merchant as fully automated systems. The double-spender generates two conflicting transactions by claiming a single output, hence double-spending it. It uses two network clients that are connected to a random set of nodes in the Bitcoin network to release the conflicting transactions. The nodes at which the transactions are released are chosen at random before each double-spending attempt in order to avoid favoring any particular configuration.

The merchant connects to a large random sample of nodes in the Bitcoin network and collects a network trace, i.e., it logs incoming transaction announcements from its peers, but does not relay any transaction in order to avoid isolating itself. The trace is used in the evaluation by selecting a random subset of the actually connected nodes, hence simulating multiple configurations and samples as they could have been observed in the real network. This allows a large number of evaluations while minimizing the number of double-spending attacks on the live

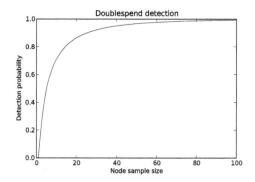

**Figure 8.2:** Probability of the merchant detecting a double-spend attempt.

network.

During the measurements 1922 double-spending attempts were initiated. The merchant was connected to 1024 nodes on average. Each additional connection causes an average of 104 bytes/second of additional bandwidth.

Although the transactions were released simultaneously and at the same number of points into the network, the ratio between the transactions observed by the merchants was not $1/2$ for either of the transactions. As soon as the balance between nodes seeing one transaction or the other is tipped to one transaction's favor, the other will be slowed down further so that the ratio the merchant observes deviates significantly from what was released into the network. The average ratio between the least distributed transaction to the most distributed transaction was 31.78%.

Furthermore, we observed that not all nodes announced transactions. Even though it is normal that nodes announce only one of the two conflicting transactions, there were nodes that did not announce either of them. On average 26.09% of peers did not announce either of the two transactions in a

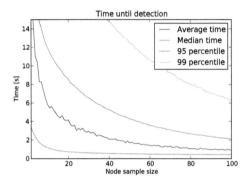

**Figure 8.3:** Average time until the merchant detects the double-spending attempt. This does not include undetected attempts (see Figure 8.2)

double-spending attempt. This lack of announcements is likely due to nodes not being up to date with the current ledger, and trying to synchronize the ledger state with the rest of the network. During the ledger synchronization the nodes do not relay incoming transactions as they might already have been confirmed.

To analyze the influence of the node sample size, we simulated the measurements by evaluating the double-spend detection repeatedly with varying subsets of the actually connected nodes. Each simulation was repeated 1000 times, resulting in 192,200,000 individual evaluations. Figure 8.2 plots the probability of the merchant eventually detecting a double-spend attempt, i.e., the probability of receiving an announcement for both conflicting transactions from its neighbors. At 100 nodes the merchant will not learn of a double-spending attempt in only 0.77% of all attempted double-spends.

As not all nodes announce transactions and we do not want to wait indefinitely until the transaction is confirmed by the network, a threshold has to be chosen after which to accept

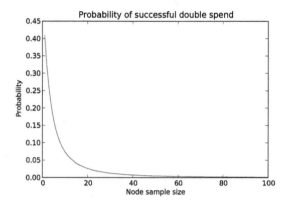

**Figure 8.4:** The probability of a double-spending attempt being successful in relation to the node sample size of the merchant.

the payment. Introducing a threshold increases the probability of accepting double-spends as it reduces the window in which we attempt to detect the double-spend. Our measurements indicate, however, that the probability of not seeing both transactions decreases exponentially with the number of announcements received. The 99 percentile for the detection of a double-spend corresponds to 37 announcements. A combination of time-based and announcement-based thresholds should yield the best result.

As can be seen from Figure 8.3 the time until the merchant detects the double-spending attack quickly decreases for larger sample sizes. The 99 percentile is at 6.29 seconds for 100 peers. Hence, we set the threshold for the announcement count to 37 and the time to 6.29 seconds. The transaction is said to be accepted if both conditions are fulfilled.

So far, we have analyzed the probability that the merchant is not aware of a double-spending attempt. However, for the double-spending attempt to be successful two additional conditions have to be met. Apart from the merchant only seeing

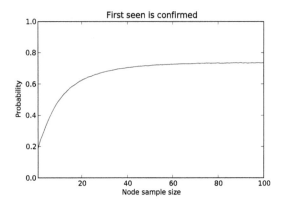

**Figure 8.5:** Probability of the first seen transaction to eventually be confirmed by the network.

one transaction, that transaction also has to be $\mathcal{T}_V$, i.e., the one that transfers the bitcoins to the merchant. Finally, $\mathcal{T}_A$, which is the transaction that transfers the bitcoins to the attacker must be the one which is later confirmed by the rest of the network. Figure 8.5 plots the probability that the transaction which is seen first by the merchant will eventually be confirmed by the Bitcoin network. With over 40 sample nodes, the probability that the first seen transaction will be confirmed is 73.64%. As we do not differentiate between $\mathcal{T}_V$ and $\mathcal{T}_A$ while sending, the probability of either being the first seen is $1/2$.

Hence, the probability of an attacker succeeding with a double-spending attempt is the product of the probabilities of the merchant first seeing $\mathcal{T}_V$, only seeing $\mathcal{T}_V$ and of $\mathcal{T}_V$ not being confirmed later. Figure 8.4 shows the probability that an attacker can successfully execute a double-spending attack against a merchant that listens to a random sample of nodes in the network. Taking into consideration the 99 percentile we used above to determine the thresholds, the attacker is left with a 0.088% chance of performing a successful double-spending attack. This means that the merchant has to hedge against a loss of one purchase in one thousand.

## 8.5 Practical Example

To test the concept of secure fast payments in a real world scenario, we realized a working system, where people can actually pay in a few seconds using bitcoins. A fitting example for a venue where fast transactions are essential is a snack vending machine where purchases are largely spontaneous impulse purchases. This impulse is significantly suppressed should the drink or candy not be dispensed immediately. The classical Bitcoin transaction confirmation scenario is thus out of place.

Our solution is divided into a verification server that connects to the Bitcoin network and manages the company wallet, and a vending machine interface that connects to the server and handles the user interaction. It is noteworthy that a single server may verify transactions for any number of clients, keeping the impact on the Bitcoin network low. The vending machine interface is implemented as an Android smartphone application as this offers a display to interact with the user, enables communication with the verification server over mobile internet and, using the IOIO prototyping platform, allows to communicate with the vending machine.

When the customer selects a product in the vending machine, the vending machine interface displays a QR-code with the payment information, such as the price and the merchant's account. The customer scans the code and issues the payment. A progress bar informs the customer about the verification progress and, upon completion, the product is dispensed.

The server provides the central interface between the Android client and the Bitcoin network. For each vending session the server submits a payment address to the client that is displayed as a QR code. Once the customer transfers the necessary funds to this address, the server starts verifying the transaction by monitoring the Bitcoin network. As soon as the fast verification is complete, the result is sent to the client (i.e. smartphone in the vending machine).

The server's wallet holds all the addresses that are generated through payment requests over time. Moreover, it has a balance of bitcoins associated to it based on the public ledger. Newly generated addresses are intended to be one-time use, which means that the wallet will register transactions to a different address each time a payment is made by a customer. One obvious reason is that it enables to track orders much easier. Another reason is aiming at anonymity, in the sense that it is not possible to easily identify the server as a major payment recipient.

For the practical implementation of the fast payment verification, the server uses a threshold $T$ to decide when the desired propagation depth has been reached. It will listen to incoming transactions to its wallet. As soon as such a transaction is first announced in the network, the server will begin to continuously monitor the transaction with respect to how many of the connected nodes in the random node sample have seen it. If the number of nodes that announced the transaction reaches $T$, the server will consider the transaction to be valid. In the meantime, should the transaction be included in the public ledger, it would immediately be considered valid by the server. In order not to keep customers waiting for too long, we considered verification times of ten seconds or less to be preferable. Based on our measurements in the Bitcoin network we chose $T = 40$ which is usually achieved in less than 10 seconds.

The vending machine is working correctly and our experiments show that not a single double-spending attack was successful against the prototype. A planned large scale test, together with the manufacturer, in Switzerland will show whether such a deployment could be successful and gauge interest in the wider public.

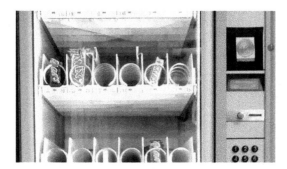

**Figure 8.6:** The snack vending machine that accepts bitcoins. Note the display on the right that can show the according QR code or transaction information.

## 8.6 Conclusion

We have shown that Bitcoin can be used as a reliable alternative for fast cashless payments. The low transaction fees of the network (compared to traditional centralized cashless payment processors) and the instant availability of the money to the merchant might render bitcoins interesting for vending machine operators.

# 9

# A Secure Bitcoin Wallet

With its growth in popularity, Bitcoin has also attracted malicious third parties trying to steal other users' bitcoins. In Bitcoin transactions, users receive bitcoins to their Bitcoin *addresses*. To spend the funds associated to a Bitcoin address, control of the corresponding *private key* is needed. Losing access to a private key is equivalent to losing the bitcoins associated to the Bitcoin address. Even though the Bitcoin system itself is protected by strong cryptography, attackers have stolen bitcoins worth millions of dollars by gaining access to the private keys of the victims. The private keys are generally stored on the computers or mobile phones of the users, where they could be exposed to malware and spyware attacks. A recent study by Litke and Stewart [52] shows that the amount of cryptocurrency-stealing malware has increased with the popularity of Bitcoin.

153

Whenever the private key is stored on a device connected to the Internet, there is a potential for theft. Our solution is to use a dedicated hardware token to store the private key needed to sign and thus authorize transactions: *BlueWallet*. This hardware token is used in combination with a device that is connected to the Bitcoin network, like the user's computer. The computer can prepare a Bitcoin transaction, but it cannot sign it. The user can use BlueWallet to review the transaction and sign it. Then, the computer can broadcast the signed transaction to the Bitcoin network. The securely stored private key never leaves the device and is only unlocked if the user correctly enters her PIN.

The hardware token delegates the creation of transactions to another entity and allows independent review of transaction details before signing. It can therefore also be used as an electronic wallet: in combination with a point of sale (POS) connected to the Bitcoin network, the device can be used to directly make Bitcoin payments. BlueWallet offers a mobile and fast solution to securing the user's bitcoins, while at the same time serving as an alternative to cash and credit cards.

## 9.1   Bitcoin

Bitcoin is an entirely digital, decentralized currency. The Bitcoin specification was introduced in 2008 by Satoshi Nakamoto [68] and a proof-of-concept client was created in 2009. Bitcoin enables instant global payments. There is no central financial authority like in traditional payment systems. Instead, the whole Bitcoin network acts as the financial authority, using cryptography to control the transfer and creation of money.

### 9.1.1   Transactions

In the Bitcoin network, a transaction describes the transfer of a specific amount of bitcoins from one individual to another. Every single Bitcoin transaction is recorded in a public ledger called the *blockchain*. A Bitcoin transaction is a digitally signed data structure that is broadcast in the Bitcoin network [30]. It consists of one ore more *inputs* and one or more *outputs*. Inputs are references to previous transactions and specify the addresses which own the bitcoins that are going to be transferred. Outputs specify the addresses that are going to receive the bitcoins, as well as the amount of bitcoins being transferred.

Each Bitcoin address is associated with a private key that is required to spend the funds assigned to the address. The Bitcoin address is derived from the public key corresponding to the private key. The user signs transactions accessing the funds of the Bitcoin address with her private key and the peers in the network verify the transaction using her public key.

To understand how Bitcoin transactions are signed and verified, it is vital to know how raw bitcoin transactions look like. Figure 9.1 gives an overview of the transaction structure as defined in the protocol specification:

- **version**: The transaction data format version, a four byte field, with default value 1.

- **tx_in[ ]**: A list of transaction inputs with **tx_in count** elements.

- **tx_out[ ]**: List of the transaction outputs with **tx_out count** elements.

- **locktime**: The block number or timestamp at which the transaction is locked. By default set to 0, meaning the transaction is immediately locked.

Each *tx_out* output element contains a destination address and the amount of bitcoins that are transferred to this address:

- **value**: Eight byte field holding the transaction value transferred to this output.

- **pkScript**: Script of length **pkScript length** containing the destination address for the bitcoins transferred to this output.

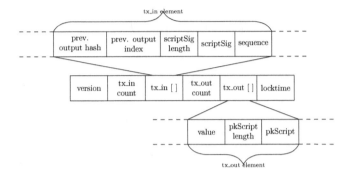

**Figure 9.1:** Transaction packet with different fields.

A *tx_in* element comprises a reference to a previous transaction's output and a script containing the signature needed to claim this output:

- **prev. output hash**: 32-byte hash of the previous transaction which is referenced in the input.

- **prev. output index**: Four byte index specifying which output of the referenced previous transaction is used as an input.

- **scriptSig**: Script of length **scriptSig length** containing the signature needed to claim the referenced output and the public key matching the address owning that output.

- **sequence**: Sequence number originally intended to allow replacement of transactions.

The *previous output hash* combined with *previous output index* points to a *pkScript* of the referenced previous transaction. This way, the address owning the bitcoins used for the input is determined.

## 9.1.2 Bitcoin Cryptography

Bitcoin uses digital signatures to ensure that bitcoins can only be spent by their owner. Ownership of bitcoins is determined by the Bitcoin addresses. The owner of a Bitcoin address holds the private key associated with this address. When creating a transaction to transfer bitcoins from this address, the owner has to prove that she has the right to do so by providing a signature created with the matching private key. As we have seen, a transaction can have multiple inputs. For a transaction to be valid, the owner must provide a valid signature for each input, thus proving that she has the rights to transfer all of the funds.

The Bitcoin protocol prescribes the use of the Elliptic Curve Digital Signature Algorithm (ECDSA) in order to sign and verify transactions. This class of cryptographic signature algorithms uses algebraic operations on elliptic curves over finite fields. The public key is derived by multiplying the base point of the curve by the private key. The base point of the curve is defined by the curve parameters. Bitcoin uses the secp256k1 curve defined in the standards for efficient cryptography [81]. The security of ECDSA depends on the fact that even though the base point and the public key are public knowledge, it is infeasible to derive the private key from this information.

The primitives provided by ECDSA are *sign()* and *verify()*. The first can be used to calculate a signature $S$ given a message $M$ and the signer's private key $p_a$, while the latter allows to verify an existing signature given the message and the public key $q_a$ of the signer.

$$S = sign(p_a, M)$$
$$verify(q_a, S, M) = \{true, false\}$$

In Bitcoin, the transaction without any signatures in the inputs is used as the message, hence the signature establishes authenticity and integrity, i.e., the transaction cannot be changed without invalidating the signature attached to the inputs:

$$S = sign(p_a, M) \wedge M' \neq M \rightarrow verify(q_a, S, M') = false$$

In order to create secure ECDSA signatures, a random parameter $k$ is necessary. It is important to select a different $k$ for each signature that is created with the same private key. Otherwise, the private key can be obtained through mathematical backtracking. For example, Sony's implementation of elliptic curve cryptography on their gaming console *Play Station 3* failed to do so, resulting in a compromised private key and full access to the system [45].

## 9.2   BlueWallet

The main purpose of BlueWallet is to sign Bitcoin transactions and thus authorize the transfer of bitcoins. In Bitcoin, transactions are usually created by the owner of the transferred bitcoins. It is however possible for another entity to prepare an unsigned transaction that tries to spend these bitcoins. While any entity may create such a transaction, only the owner of the bitcoins can provide the signatures needed to authorize the transaction.

By delegating the preparation of the unsigned transaction to another entity, BlueWallet does not have to be connected to the Bitcoin network. This allows us to build a device with a low power consumption and with small memory requirements. The user's private key needed to sign a transaction is safely stored on BlueWallet. The private key never leaves BlueWallet and is only unlocked if the user correctly enters her PIN.

There are two applications for BlueWallet. Firstly, it can be used in combination with the user's home computer or smart phone, similar to e-banking solutions. The user can create a Bitcoin transaction on a device which is connected to the Bitcoin network and use BlueWallet to sign it. The private key needed to access the user's funds is no longer stored on her personal computer or smart phone, which is compromised more easily.

The second application is fundamentally different from the first. The transaction is created by an untrusted third party and BlueWallet acts as an electronic wallet. An example of this third party could be the POS in a store, a restaurant or any other place where one would normally pay with cash, debit or credit card. Since the transaction is created by an untrusted party, additional security measures have to be implemented in BlueWallet to minimize the risk incurred by the user. In addition to the signing ability of BlueWallet, the user may review and authorize the transaction independently from the POS and BlueWallet has to ensure that only the authorized bitcoins are transferred.

We will subsequently focus on the second application since it is more challenging. If BlueWallet manages to meet all the necessary requirements for the use with an untrusted POS, it can be used in conjunction with a computer or smart phone owned by the user.

### 9.2.1 Creating a Transaction

Assuming a customer in a shop intends to make a payment to the POS using BlueWallet. The POS is connected to the Bitcoin network and will be tasked with the creation of the unsigned payment transaction. In order for the POS to create the transaction, it first needs to learn the customer's address. This is the address whose corresponding private key is stored in the BlueWallet. The POS therefore contacts the BlueWallet and retrieves the address.

Once the POS has the customer's address it scans its local copy of the transaction history for outputs that may be claimed by the address, i.e., earlier transactions that funded the address. The POS will then create a transaction incrementally selecting the found outputs until the desired amount is covered and adding inputs referencing them in the payment transaction. Table 9.1 shows an example of an unsigned transaction in the same format as it would be transferred from the POS to the BlueWallet. Two outputs are added to the transaction, one transferring the payment amount to the POS, destined to the POS' address (*tx_out[1]*), and the other totaling the remaining bitcoins that are sent back to the address of the BlueWallet (*tx_out[0]*). Should the POS be unable to locate enough outputs to claim the desired amount, it will return an error and abort the transaction creation.

The transaction will be completed by adding the default values for the locktime (0 to lock the transaction immediately) and the sequence in the inputs (`0xffffffff` to disallow replacement). It should be noted that the signature fields scriptSig length and scriptSig are set to an empty string with length 0.

Once the unsigned transaction is created, the POS will contact the BlueWallet and transfer the previous transactions as well as the newly created unsigned transaction.

### 9.2.2   Unsigned Transaction Verification

Since BlueWallet does not have any connection to the Bitcoin network, it has to take precautions to make sure that the untrusted POS has created a correct transaction.

Once an output has been referenced in a confirmed transaction it is marked as claimed and cannot be claimed again. This means that the entire value associated with an output is always spent in the claiming transaction. This is why bitcoin transactions usually have at least two outputs. One for the address to which a certain amount of bitcoins shall be transferred, and one returning the remaining funds as a new output.

If we have an untrusted party like the POS creating the transaction for us, this could be an issue. If we take a look at a the raw transaction illustrated in Table 9.1, we observe that the value of an input is not stated in Bitcoin transactions. Therefore, BlueWallet cannot infer the value of the inputs only from the unsigned transaction the POS sent to BlueWallet. Since we do not know how many of our bitcoins are going to be transferred, we would have to rely on the POS to return the correct amount of bitcoins back to our address.

The value of the inputs is usually determined by looking at

| version | | 01 00 00 00 |
|---|---|---|
| tx_in count | | 01 |
| tx_in[0] | prev. output hash | 13 cb 3b 56 7d ef 7f fa dc aa 69 de 20 cb 19 09 00 29 02 8b 05 d8 a9 73 d1 5d b5 cf 43 37 a5 a1 |
| | prev. output index | 00 00 00 00 |
| | scriptSig length | 00 |
| | scriptSig | <empty> |
| | sequence | ff ff ff ff |
| tx_out count | | 02 |
| tx_out[0] | value | c0 2a 99 1c 00 00 00 00 |
| | pkScript length | 19 |
| | pkScript | 76 a9 14 29 4f db f5 26 0a be 18 48 9b 48 07 f7 ba f0 62 07 70 c3 b7 88 ac |
| tx_out[1] | value | 80 96 98 00 00 00 00 00 |
| | pkScript length | 19 |
| | pkScript | 76 a9 14 8e e6 7a 65 55 28 b6 1d e2 29 f4 5f c0 16 a0 0f 08 f3 cc 32 88 ac |
| locktime | | 00 00 00 00 |

**Table 9.1:** The complete unsigned transaction as prepared by the POS.

the outputs of the referenced previous transactions. However, BlueWallet is not connected to the Bitcoin network and cannot look up the previous transactions on its own. Therefore, the POS is required to also send us all of the prior transactions that are referenced in the inputs of the current transactions. By looking at the outputs of the prior transactions, BlueWallet can determine the sum of all inputs, i.e., how many bitcoins we are going to transfer. BlueWallet compares this sum to the total value of all the outputs. The value of the bitcoins returned to us should be the sum of all our inputs minus the amount of bitcoins transferred to the POS minus an acceptable transaction fee.

BlueWallet, however, has no way to verify that the previous transactions the POS sent were confirmed by the Bitcoin network. How can we make sure the POS did not just change the output values in the prior transactions it sent BlueWallet? To check the correctness of prior transactions, BlueWallet hashes all the received prior transactions. These hashes are compared to the *previous output hashes* in the inputs of the current transaction.

If all the hashes match, we know that the POS sent unmodified prior transactions. Even one single byte-change in a prior transaction would lead to a completely different hash, and thus a rejection of the current transaction.

But what if the POS changed the *previous output hashes* in the current transaction in order to match the hashes of the modified previous transactions? In that case, BlueWallet accepts the current transaction. The Bitcoin network, however, would reject the transaction, since the modified *previous output hashes* do not reference existing prior transactions. In the end, the POS would not receive any bitcoins at all.

This is a strong incentive for the POS to send us the correct prior transactions and to return the correct amount of bitcoins to our address.

### 9.2.3   Signing Transactions

Creating the required signatures to authorize a transaction is a rather involved process. To sign a transaction, the owner of the transferred bitcoins has to create a valid signature for every one of the inputs. To create a valid signature for an input, the following steps have to be taken.

First, BlueWallet creates a temporary copy of the unsigned transaction, which is needed to generate the signature. This temporary copy is then modified. The *scriptSig* of the input we want to create the signature for has to be filled with the *pkScript* of the referenced output we want to claim. Remember, the input references a previous transaction's output and this output contains a *pkScript*. This *pkScript* includes the Bitcoin address which owns the output.

Since the output of the previous transaction is owned by the BlueWallet's Bitcoin address, this is a *pkScript* containing our Bitcoin address. The *pkScript* is exactly the same for all outputs owned by our address. In this case, we already encountered it in Table 9.1. It is included in the transaction change output, since this output will also be owned by our address.

In order to create the signature for the input, BlueWallet replaces *scriptSig* of *tx_in[0]* in Table 9.1 with the *pkScript* containing our Bitcoin address, and updates *scriptSig length*.

Before BlueWallet can create the signature, it will have to append a so called *hash type* field to the copy of the unsigned transaction. The default value of this four byte field is 1. This *hash type* is called *SIGHASH_ALL* and indicates that all the outputs are signed. Therefore, each output can only be claimed by its rightful owner. There are also other hash types, but they are not relevant to our use-case.

The modified copy of the unsigned transaction is now double-SHA256 hashed, and the resulting hash is signed with the private key corresponding to our Bitcoin address. The result is a DER-encoded signature [32]. To this signature a one-byte *hash type* has to be added. As the name suggests *scriptSig* is a script that wraps the DER-encoded signature. It starts with a byte indicating the length of the DER-encoded signature including the hashtype-byte. This is followed by the signature and the hashtype-byte itself. Next comes one byte containing the length of the public key. Finally, the public key is added.

In case the transaction has more than one input, a signature has to be created for every single input. This is done one signature at a time. For every signature a copy of the unsigned transaction is created and only the *scriptSig* of the input we want to create the signature for is temporarily filled with the corresponding *pkScript*. The other inputs are left as is, with empty *scriptSig*.

The valid signed transaction is then created by adding the

*scriptSig* generated with the modified copy of the unsigned transaction to the original unsigned transaction shown in Table 9.1. The empty *scriptSig* field is replaced by the newly generated *scriptSig*, and the *scriptSig length* field is updated accordingly.

### 9.2.4   Verifying Transactions

Once all signatures have been added to the transaction, it is sent back to the POS, which will then verify the transaction's validity.

The POS has to check that its address and the correct value is still listed in the outputs of the signed transaction it received from the BlueWallet. To verify a Bitcoin transaction, its signatures have to be verified. The necessary steps to verify a signature are similar to the steps taken to create a signature. From the signed transaction a transaction equal to the modified copy of the unsigned transaction has to be created. This transaction is then also double-SHA256 hashed, which will lead to the hash that was originally used to create the signature. Using a cryptographic verification algorithm and the public key from the signed transaction, it can now be determined, whether the signature was created from this hash.

If the transaction is not valid, the POS is not going to receive any bitcoins, since the transaction would be rejected by the Bitcoin network. In case the transaction is invalid, the POS aborts the payment process.

If the transaction is found to be valid, the POS releases it into the Bitcoin network. The transaction is verified by other peers and eventually confirmed by the Bitcoin network. A transaction is confirmed when it ends up in the blockchain, the public ledger of the Bitcoin network. This process may take between 10 and 40 minutes. Since waiting this long to complete the payment process is neither in the interest of the POS nor the customer, the POS will have to accept so-called fast payments [47]. Here, the POS does not wait for confirmation by the Bitcoin network. It accepts payments as soon as it sees the transaction being forwarded in the network. Fast payments build upon trusting a transaction to be eventually confirmed by the network. But this might not always be the case.

By accepting fast payments the POS becomes susceptible to double-spend attempts. A double-spend attempt is an attack where the attacker tries to acquire a good or service from a merchant without paying for it. From the POS' view, we could be such an attacker. Our double-spend attempt would include the following steps. Upon receiving the unsigned transaction by the POS, we create a second transaction using the same previous outputs as inputs. The second transaction may transfer the bitcoins to another address, which could be our own. We then sign the original transaction and send it to the POS. If we manage to release the second transaction into the Bitcoin network at the same time, it will be verified by peers in the network and could later be confirmed by the Bitcoin network. Since outputs can only be spent once, the transaction that is supposed to pay the POS will then eventually be rejected by the network. By then, we would have long left the store with the goods.

In order to prevent such double-spend attacks, the POS constantly monitors the Bitcoin network for other transactions spending the outputs chosen for the payment transaction. Furthermore, to secure fast payments the POS could implement the techniques described by [14]. The POS is always connected to a large amount of other peers in the network. For a fast payment transaction to be accepted, a certain percentage of the connected peers must have seen the transaction after a couple of seconds.

## 9.3 Implementation

In this section, we illustrate how we created a prototype of BlueWallet with the previously mentioned capabilities.

Figure 9.2 illustrates the POS scenario and shows the main components of BlueWallet. For communication with the POS

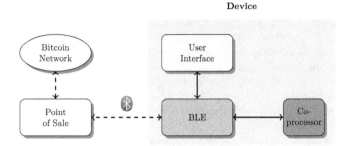

**Figure 9.2:** System overview with contributing components.

BlueWallet incorporates a Bluetooth Low Energy (BLE) module. Compared to classic Bluetooth it provides a considerably reduced power consumption. To process and sign transactions quickly and to improve security, BlueWallet features a co-processor. This co-processor consumes more power than the other parts of the system and therefore immediately enters the stand-by mode whenever it is not used.

### 9.3.1   BlueWallet Prototype

The user interface of BlueWallet consists of an OLED display and four buttons. The display is used to show relevant information to the user, the buttons are required for user input. The four buttons are placed next to the four corners of the display. On the right side of the display, we have an *OK* button, used to confirm user input and transactions and a *CANCEL* button, used to cancel user input and reject transactions. On the left side of the display, there is an *UP* and a *DOWN* button, used for selection purposes and for choosing the digits when entering the PIN code.

The Bluetooth Low Energy module is a Bluegiga BLE113 with integrated microcontroller and Bluetooth radio. The Bluetooth Low Energy module is the heart of BlueWallet. It is

| UUID | Properties | Description |
|------|-----------|-------------|
| 0xfff1 | read | Public key of the device's owner |
| 0xfff2 | read | Signed transaction |
| 0xfff3 | write | Unsigned transaction |
| 0xfff4 | write | New public & private key |
| 0xfff5 | read | Device state |
| 0xfff6 | write | POS state |
| 0xfff7 | write | Prior transactions |

**Table 9.2:** GATT characteristics of the Blue Wallet application.

capable of communicating over Bluetooth Low Energy with the POS, interfaces with the microcontroller needed for cryptographic calculations, reacts to user input and controls the display.

The integrated microcontroller in the BLE113 is a 8-bit CC2541 by Texas Instruments. It is a power-optimized chip for BLE applications. The BlueWallet application running on the CC2541 chip is the major building block of our device and implements the state machine, which handles the different states of BlueWallet. It was developed using the BLE software development platform by Texas Instruments.

For data communication with the POS, BlueWallet uses the Generic Attribute (GATT) layer of the BLE protocol stack. Using a *GATT profile* BlueWallet is able to provide access to GATT *characteristics*. These characteristics contain values that can be written and read by a connected device, depending on the characteristics' properties. The customized GATT profile that we designed for data exchange between BlueWallet and the POS is shown in Table 9.2. Each characteristic has a Bluetooth UUID (universal unique identifier) which is needed to access it.

In order to sign transactions, BlueWallet requires more computational resources than the CC2541 could provide. Initial tests with an implementation of ECDSA on this power-saving chip resulted in run-times for a single signature of over 90 sec-

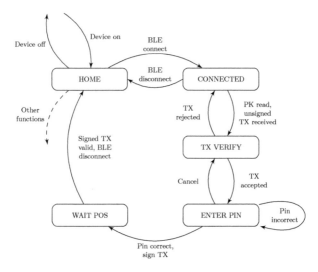

**Figure 9.3:** The important states for the payment process.

onds, which might be acceptable for non time critical scenarios such as e-Banking, but not for the POS scenario.

Thus, BlueWallet features an STM32F205RE co-processor (STM), a 32-bit microcontroller by STMicroelectronics, that is used for all cryptographic operations. It provides approximately two orders of magnitude speedup, verifying and signing transactions with one input in under a second.

Moreover, by separating the cryptographic domain from the Bluetooth domain, we can improve the overall security of Blue-Wallet. By only storing the private key needed for signature generation on the STM, we can make sure that even if the Bluetooth connection is compromised the private key is not. Eventually we will use a tamper resistant cryptoprocessor, so that even physical access to BlueWallet would not give access to the encrypted private key. At the time of writing no such processor exists due to the choice of the secp256k1 curve in the

Bitcoin protocol.

The BLE113 and the STM communicate over UART via a direct connection. In addition, the BLE113 has the ability to wake up the STM from standby mode. This is necessary because the STM has a significantly higher power consumption when in run mode. The typical supply current when the chip is clocked at 120 MHz lies between 33 and 61 mA. In standby mode the chip only draws around 4 $\mu$A. Since BlueWallet is powered by a battery, we generally want to use as little power as possible and thus make use of the standby mode of the STM. The application running on the STM implements the Bitcoin signature scheme described in Section 9.2.3. It acts like a simple state machine that only reacts to commands and data it receives from the BLE113.

Figure 9.3 shows the important states for the payment process. Upon starting BlueWallet, the state machine enters the *HOME* state. BlueWallet is now advertising over Bluetooth and the POS is able to establish a Bluetooth Low Energy connection. When a new payment process is started, the POS connects to BlueWallet and the state machine switches to the *CONNECTED* state.

The POS reads the public key of the BlueWallet's owner (characteristic `0xfff1`) and builds the unsigned transaction as specified in Section 9.2.1. Once the *device state* (`0xfff5`) indicates that BlueWallet is ready to receive data the POS sends the unsigned (`0xfff3`) and the corresponding prior transactions (`0xfff7`). The BLE113 forwards the transactions to the STM which verifies the unsigned and the prior transactions and sends the transaction information back.

The state machine switches to the *TX VERIFY* state and BlueWallet displays the transaction information to the user. In addition to the automatic verification of the unsigned transaction that is done by the STM, the user has to manually confirm the correctness of the transaction. Looking at the display, she can verify the address she is going to transfer bitcoins to, the amount of bitcoins that are transferred and also check the transaction fee.

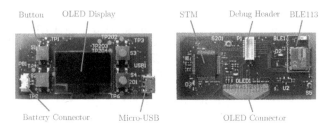

**Figure 9.4:** The top and bottom views of the PCB.

If the transaction information is correct, the user accepts the transaction and the state machine switches to the *ENTER PIN* state. Each transaction has to be authorized by the owner of BlueWallet with her PIN. This ensures that, even when Blue-Wallet is lost or stolen, a third party is unable to make payments.

Upon entering the PIN, the BLE113 instructs the STM to sign the transaction. The STM signs the unsigned transaction with the user's private key and returns the signed transaction. The BLE113's state machine switches to the *WAIT POS* state. Now that the signed transaction is ready, which is again signaled by the device state characteristic, the POS reads the signed transaction (`0xfff2`) and uses the user's public key to verify it. If everything is in order, the POS informs BlueWallet that the payment has been accepted by writing the *POS state* (`0xfff6`) characteristic and closes the Bluetooth connection. This causes the state machine to return to the *HOME* state.

For the BlueWallet prototype we created a printed circuit board (PCB) which physically supports and connects all the components. The size of the PCB is restricted by the size of our final device. There are several constraints for the size of the device: the display needs to be large enough to accommodate the necessary information and the buttons should be easily reachable, yet BlueWallet should be small enough to be carried around by the user. The PCB for the prototype has a size of 65 x 30 mm. The buttons and the display are placed on the top of the PCB, whereas the two microcontrollers and most of the other electrical components are located on the bottom of the PCB.

To determine how much current BlueWallet would draw at most, we summed up the maximum supply currents of the two microcontrollers and the OLED display. The OLED display has a maximum operating current of 28.9 mA, the BLE113 needs 18.2mA and the STM 61mA at most [17, 82, 85]. This results in a total maximum supply current needed for BlueWallet of 108.1mA. Therefore, we chose a lithium polymer battery with a capacity of 110mAh to power BlueWallet. This way, BlueWallet will at least run one hour before having to be charged again. A payment process does generally not take longer than 30 seconds. Thus, a user can complete around 100 payment processes before having to charge BlueWallet again. It should be noted that we looked at the maximum operating current of each component. Generally, each component should draw less current resulting in an even longer battery life.

Eventually, the battery will be discharged. To provide the user with a simple way of recharging the battery, we added a micro-USB connector and a battery charger circuit to BlueWallet.

For the prototype, we chose a multi-layer PCB with four layers. It consists of the top and the bottom layer which will hold the electrical components, a power plane, and a ground plane. Components can be connected to these planes using through-hole vias.

The bottom layer of the PCB with the components in place is shown in Figure 9.4. It should be noted that even though the display is located on the top layer of the PCB, the pads to connect the display are placed on the bottom layer. The display's pins are located on a flexible flat cable. The cable is soldered to the pads on the bottom layer of the PCB and then bent around the edge of the PCB. As a result, the display will come to rest on the top layer of the PCB.

**Figure 9.5:** The final device including the case for the printed circuit board.

On the top layer illustrated in Figure 9.4, there are only a few electrical components. Soldered to the top layer are the four buttons, the micro-USB port needed for charging the battery and a 2-pin connector for the battery.

Evaluating the prototype, we found that it takes approximately 1.5 seconds to send the unsigned transaction and one previous transaction to BlueWallet. Upon receiving the transaction details, they are displayed almost instantly by BlueWallet. A thorough review of the transaction details can be done in about 10 seconds. The time it takes to enter the PIN code depends on the length of the PIN code, but generally does not take longer than 10 seconds. The co-processor signs a transaction in less than one second. Then, it again takes around 1.5 seconds to return the signed transaction to the POS. A complete payment process at a POS should therefore take around 20 seconds.

### 9.3.2   Point of Sale

To test the BlueWallet in the POS scenario, we implemented the POS on a computer using a CSR 4.0 USB dongle to for Bluetooth Low Energy communication. To establish a connection with the Bitcoin network, our POS uses *bitcoind*, a variant of the reference client. The bitcoind client provides a JSON-RPC

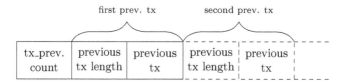

**Figure 9.6:** Previous transactions serialized by the point of sale.

API. Our POS application makes use of this RPC interface and is also able to access the Bluetooth Low Energy functions of the USB dongle.

When the POS has established the connection to BlueWallet and read our Bitcoin address, it uses bitcoind to look up the balance of the address and find possible outputs of previous transactions associated to this address that can be used as inputs for the new transaction. With this information it creates the new unsigned transaction. Furthermore, for each input the POS has to send the complete previous transaction to BlueWallet. The POS serializes the previous transactions as illustrated in Figure 9.6. The total number of previous transactions is followed by the first previous transaction. If there is more than one input in the unsigned transaction, the POS adds the additional previous transactions as well. This data is written to the *prior transaction* characteristic of BlueWallet. Then, the POS sends the unsigned transaction to BlueWallet.

To know when BlueWallet has signed the transaction, the POS subscribes to the *device state* characteristic. The POS will be notified by BlueWallet when the characteristic changes its value. If the value indicates that the transaction has been signed, the POS reads the *signed transaction* characteristic. Then, again using bitcoind, the POS verifies the correctness of the signed transaction and sends it to the Bitcoin network.

## 9.4   Related Work

The security of using Bitcoins for fast payment scenarios, like using Bitcoin at a point of sale, where payment confirmation is required immediately, was first analyzed by Karame et al. [47]. The use of Bitcoin at a point of sale using near field communication to exchange payment information with a smart phone was examined by Bronleewe [21]. A proof of concept for a point of sale scenario implementing and expanding upon fast payment security was developed by Bamert et al. [14].

The increase of malware attacks on Bitcoin clients resulting in compromised private keys and theft of bitcoins is discussed by Barber et al. [15]. An analysis of German and US law with regards to theft of bitcoins was conducted by Boehm et al. [18]. They found that traditional criminal law is not well equipped to handle the theft of virtual goods. These findings show that it is vital to protect private keys. Litke and Stewart describe the best practices for storing private keys, including hardware tokens [53]. The benefits of hardware tokens supporting public-key cryptography with regards to e-banking are discussed by Hiltgen [42].

An approach to public-key cryptography called elliptic curve cryptography was proposed independently by Koblitz [49] and Miller [61]. Elliptic curve cryptography is the foundation for the Elliptic Curve Digital Signature Algorithm (ECDSA) which is used by the Bitcoin protocol to sign transactions and is described in detail by Johnson and Menezes [44]. A review of ECDSA in practice to reveal vulnerabilities was done by Bos et al. [19]. They found that repeated per-message signature secrets led to compromised private keys of Bitcoin users.

The benefits of Bluetooth Low Energy when it comes to low energy devices are described by Gomez et al. [40]. Kamath and Lindh measure Bluetooth Low Energy power consumption of a CC2541 chip by Texas Instruments [46].

## 9.5 Conclusion

BlueWallet can be used to sign and authorize transactions that are created by the user's computer or smart phone. Using Bluetooth Low Energy to communicate with the entity creating the unsigned transaction we were able to build a device that features a low power consumption and thus is well equipped to be used on the go. Furthermore, by delegating the creation of the unsigned transaction to another entity BlueWallet can directly be used as an electronic wallet in combination with a point of sale. Implementing several security precautions, BlueWallet makes sure that transactions created by an untrusted point of sale can be used to make Bitcoin payments in a store. We found that signing Bitcoin transactions with BlueWallet is secure and fast. A user can simply pay with Bitcoin by reviewing the transaction information on the screen of BlueWallet and entering her PIN code. Therefore, our electronic wallet is a viable alternative to card based payment methods and cash.

# 10

# Conclusion

It has been just over 7 years since Bitcoin was released to the public, and it had an undeniable impact on our daily lives. As part of the FinTech movement it has disrupted the way our financial system works, starting a movement to modernize and increase efficiency. A remarkable feat given that the consumer facing financial industry has been mostly stagnant over the last century. While other sectors embraced the technological advances, financial services have always been wary of change.

In these years Bitcoin has changed from a small network run by a few enthusiasts, to a network that counts thousands of nodes and supports a multi-billion industry. The underlying technology however has not changed and, while still revolutionary, the changing requirements are starting to expose some problems.

We set out to address two of these problems, namely we

wanted to see whether Bitcoin scales and investigate its security. We found that the Bitcoin protocol does not scale well and is likely to hit its limits soon. We have then proposed two potential solutions in the form of Duplex Micropayment Channels and PeerCensus. Duplex Micropayment Channels move a vast majority of transfers off the blockchain, the central bottleneck in today's Bitcoin, and use it for conflict resolution. On the other hand PeerCensus attempts to abstract the blockchain in such a way that it is no longer bound to a single application, enabling multiple applications to share a single blockchain, thus eliminating resource contention among application. Both systems provide real-time, durable, transfers.

For the security question we investigated what security guarantees Bitcoin provides out of the box, how end-users can secure their funds and how the blockchain can be used to create an audit without trusted intermediaries. We have shown how a fiduciary can prove its liquidity without revealing its assets and its liabilities and the MtGox incident has shown how the public transaction history can be used to investigate an alleged theft.

Bitcoin and the underlying blockchain truly are disruptive technologies, which are no longer confined solely to finance. As a Bitcoin early adopter and researcher it is my hope that Bitcoin and blockchain technology in general have a bright future and that with this work I could contribute to further the understanding of their potential as well as their limitations, and show how these limitations can be overcome.

# Bibliography

[1] : Bitcoin virtual currency: Unique features present distinct challenges for deterring illicit activity. Technical report, Federal Bureau of Investigation (2012)

[2] : Virtual currency schemes. Technical report, European Central Bank (2012)

[3] : Application of fincen's regulations to persons administering, exchanging, or using virtual currencies. Technical report, Financial Crimes Enforcement Network, US Department of the Treasury (2013)

[4] Andreesen, G.: BIP 0050: March 2013 Chain Fork Post-Mortem. `https://github.com/bitcoin/bips` (2013) [Online; accessed December 12, 2014].

[5] Andresen, G.: Bitcoin improvement proposal 11: M-of-N standard transactions. `https://github.com/bitcoin/bips/blob/master/bip-0011.mediawiki` (2011, Online; accessed February, 2015)

[6] Androulaki, E., Karame, G., Roeschlin, M., Scherer, T., Capkun, S.: Evaluating user privacy in bitcoin. IACR Cryptology ePrint Archive **2012** (2012) 596

[7] Andrychowicz, M., Dziembowski, S., Malinowski, D., Mazurek, Ł.: Fair two-party computations via the bitcoin deposits. Technical report, Cryptology ePrint Archive (2013)

[8] Andrychowicz, M., Dziembowski, S., Malinowski, D., Mazurek, L.: How to deal with malleability of bitcoin transactions. arXiv preprint arXiv:1312.3230 (2013)

[9] Araoz, M., Charles, R.X., Garcia, M.A.: Bip 45: Structure for deterministic P2SH multisignature wallets. https://github.com/bitcoin/bips/blob/master/bip-0045.mediawiki (2014, Online; accessed February, 2015)

[10] Babaioff, M., Dobzinski, S., Oren, S., Zohar, A.: On bitcoin and red balloons. In: Proc. of Electronic Commerce. (2012)

[11] Back, A.: Hashcash — a denial of service counter-measure. URL: http://www.hashcash.org/papers/hashcash.pdf (2002)

[12] Back, A., Bentov, I.: Note on fair coin toss via bitcoin. arXiv preprint arXiv:1402.3698 (2014)

[13] Back, A., Corallo, M., Dashjr, L., Friedenbach, M., Maxwell, G., Miller, A., Poelstra, A., Timón, J., Wuille, P.: Enabling blockchain innovations with pegged sidechains (2014)

[14] Bamert, T., Decker, C., Elsen, L., Welten, S., Wattenhofer, R.: Have a snack, pay with bitcoin. In: IEEE Internation Conference on Peer-to-Peer Computing (P2P), Trento, Italy. (2013)

[15] Barber, S., Boyen, X., Shi, E., Uzun, E.: Bitter to better—how to make bitcoin a better currency. Financial Cryptography and Data Security (2012)

[16] Becker, J., Breuker, D., Heide, T., Holler, J., Rauer, H.P., Böhme, R.: Geld stinkt, bitcoin auch — eine Ökobilanz der bitcoin block chain. In: BTC 2012: Workshop Bitcoin

[17] Bluegiga: BLE113 datasheet v1.2 (2013) [Online, Retrieved March, 2014].

[18] Boehm, F., Pesch, P.: Bitcoin: A First Legal Analysis - with Reference to German and American Law. In: Workshop on Bitcoin Research. (2014)

[19] Bos, J.W., Halderman, J.A., Heninger, N., Moore, J., Naehrig, M., Wustrow, E.: Elliptic curve cryptography in practice. Microsoft Research. November (2013)

[20] Brito, J., Castillo, A.: Bitcoin: A primer for policymakers. Mercatus Center at George Mason University (2013)

[21] Bronleewe, D.A.: Bitcoin NFC. Technical report, University of Texas (2011)

[22] Bryans, D.: Bitcoin and money laundering: mining for an effective solution. Indiana Law Journal (2014)

[23] Butterin, V., et al.: A next-generation smart contract and decentralized application platform (2014)

[24] Castro, M., Liskov, B., et al.: A correctness proof for a practical byzantine-fault-tolerant replication algorithm. Technical report, Technical Memo MIT/LCS/TM-590, MIT Laboratory for Computer Science (1999)

[25] Castro, M., Liskov, B., et al.: Practical byzantine fault tolerance. In: OSDI. Volume 99. (1999) 173–186

[26] Chaum, D.: Blind signatures for untraceable payments. In: Advances in cryptology. (1983)

[27] Chaum, D., Fiat, A., Naor, M.: Untraceable electronic cash. In: Advances in cryptology. (1990)

[28] Clark, J., Essex, A.: Commitcoin: Carbon dating commitments with bitcoin. In: Financial Cryptography and Data Security. (2012)

[29] Decker, C., Seidel, J., Wattenhofer, R.: Bitcoin meets strong consistency. arXiv preprint arXiv:1412.7935 (2014)

[30] Decker, C., Wattenhofer, R.: Information propagation in the bitcoin network. In: IEEE International Conference on Peer-to-Peer Computing (P2P), Trento, Italy. (September 2013)

[31] Decker, C., Wattenhofer, R.: Bitcoin Transaction Malleability and MtGox. In: 19th European Symposium on Research in Computer Security (ESORICS), Wroclaw, Poland. (September 2014)

[32] Dubuisson, O.: ASN. 1: communication between heterogeneous systems. Morgan Kaufmann (2001)

[33] Dwork, C., Naor, M.: Pricing via processing or combating junk mail. Lecture Notes in Computer Science **576** (1992) 114–128

[34] Dwork, C., Naor, M.: Pricing via processing or combatting junk mail. In: Advances in Cryptology

[35] Elias, M.: Bitcoin: Tempering the digital ring of gyges or implausible pecuniary privacy. Available at SSRN 1937769 (2011)

[36] Eyal, I., Sirer, E.G.: Majority is not enough: Bitcoin mining is vulnerable. arXiv preprint arXiv:1311.0243 (2013)

[37] Finney, H.: bcflick - using TPM's and trusted computing to strengthen bitcoin wallets. https://bitcointalk.org/index.php?topic=154290.msg1635481 (2013 (Online; accessed February, 2015))

[38] Garay, J., Kiayias, A., Leonardos, N.: The bitcoin back-bone protocol: Analysis and applications. Technical report (2014)

[39] Gerhardt, I., Hanke, T.: Homomorphic payment addresses and the pay-to-contract protocol. CoRR **abs/1212.3257** (2012)

[40] Gomez, C., Oller, J., Paradells, J.: Overview and evaluation of Bluetooth Low Energy: An emerging low-power wireless technology. Sensors (2012)

[41] Hearn, M., Spilman, J.: Bitcoin contracts. `https://en.bitcoin.it/wiki/Contracts` [Online; accessed May 2015].

[42] Hiltgen, A., Kramp, T., Weigold, T.: Secure internet banking authentication. Security & Privacy (2006)

[43] Intel Corporation: Intel Trusted Execution Technology Software Developers Guide. (May 2014)

[44] Johnson, D., Menezes, A., Vanstone, S.: The elliptic curve digital signature algorithm (ECDSA). International Journal of Information Security (2001)

[45] Jonathan Fildes: PS3 ECDSA security failure. `http://www.bbc.co.uk/news/technology-12116051` [Online, Retrieved March, 2014].

[46] Kamath, S., Lindh, J.: Measuring Bluetooth Low Energy power consumption. Texas instruments application note AN092, Dallas (2010)

[47] Karame, G., Androulaki, E., Capkun, S.: Two Bitcoins at the Price of One? Double-Spending Attacks on Fast Payments in Bitcoin. In: Proc. of Conference on Computer and Communication Security. (2012)

[48] Karp, R., Schindelhauer, C., Shenker, S., Vocking, B.: Randomized rumor spreading. In: Proc. of Foundations of Computer Science. (2000)

[49] Koblitz, N.: Elliptic curve cryptosystems. Mathematics of computation (1987)

[50] Kotla, R., Alvisi, L., Dahlin, M., Clement, A., Wong, E.: Zyzzyva: speculative byzantine fault tolerance. In: ACM SIGOPS symposium on Operating systems principles. (2007)

[51] Lamport, L., Shostak, R., Pease, M.: The byzantine generals problem. ACM Transactions on Programming Languages and Systems (1982)

[52] Litke, P., Stewart, J.: Cryptocurrency-stealing malware landscape. Technical report, Technical report, Dell SecureWorks Counter Threat Unit (2014)

[53] Litke, P., Stewart, J.: Enterprise best practices for cryptocurrency adoption (2014) [Online, Retrieved March, 2014].

[54] Maxwell, G., Todd, P.: Fraud proof. `https://people.xiph.org/~greg/bitcoin-wizards-fraud-proof.log.txt` (2013 (Online; accessed March, 2015))

[55] Maxwell, G., Wilcox, Z.: Proving your bitcoin reserves. `https://iwilcox.me.uk/2014/proving-bitcoin-reserves` (2014 (Online; accessed January 5th, 2015))

[56] McCune, J.M., Parno, B.J., Perrig, A., Reiter, M.K., Isozaki, H.: Flicker: An execution infrastructure for TCB minimization. In: ACM SIGOPS Operating Systems Review. (2008)

[57] Merkle, R.C.: A digital signature based on a conventional encryption function. In: Advances in Cryptology. (1988)

[58] Miers, I., Garman, C., Green, M., Rubin, A.D.: Zerocoin: Anonymous distributed e-cash from bitcoin. (2013)

[59] Miller, A., LaViola, J.: Anonymous byzantine consensus from moderately-hard puzzles: A model for bitcoin. (2014)

[60] Miller, A., Shi, E., Kosba, A., Katz, J.: Preprint: Nonoutsourceable scratch-off puzzles to discourage bitcoin mining coalitions

[61] Miller, V.S.: Use of elliptic curves in cryptography. In: Advances in Cryptology-CRYPTO'85. (1986)

[62] Mitzenmacher, M., Upfal, E.: Probability and computing: Randomized algorithms and probabilistic analysis. Cambridge University Press (2005)

[63] Moore, T., Christin, N.: Beware the middleman: Empirical analysis of bitcoin-exchange risk. In: Financial Cryptography and Data Security. (2013)

[64] MtGox: Announcement regarding an application for commencement of a prodedure of civil rehabilitation. `https://www.mtgox.com/img/pdf/20140228-announcement_eng.pdf` [Online; accessed March 19th].

[65] MtGox: Announcement regarding the applicability of us bankruptcy code chapter 15. `https://www.mtgox.com/img/pdf/20140314-announcement_chapter15.pdf` [Online; accessed March 19th].

[66] MtGox: Mtgox press release about transaction malleability. `https://www.mtgox.com/press_release_20140210.html` (2014) [Online; accessed February 10th, 2014].

[67] MtGox: Mtgox press release announcing the stop of withdrawals. `https://www.mtgox.com/press_release_20140210.html` (2014) [Online; accessed February 10th, 2014].

[68] Nakamoto, S.: Bitcoin: A peer-to-peer electronic cash system. `https://bitcoin.org/bitcoin.pdf` [Online; accessed March 26, 2014].

[69] Nakamoto, S.: Bitcoin p2p e-cash paper. http://www.mail-archive.com/cryptography@metzdowd.com/msg09959.html (2008) [Online; accessed January, 2013].

[70] New York State Department of Financial Services: Virtual Currencies. `http://www.dfs.ny.gov/legal/regulations/revised_vc_regulation.pdf` (2015 (Online; accessed February, 2015))

[71] Pease, M., Shostak, R., Lamport, L.: Reaching agreement in the presence of faults. Journal of the ACM (JACM)

[72] Poon, J., Dryja, T.: The bitcoin lightning network

[73] Reid, F., Harrigan, M.: An analysis of anonymity in the bitcoin system. In: Proc. of the Conference on Social Computing (socialcom). (2011)

[74] Reiter, M.K.: A secure group membership protocol. Transactions on Software Engineering (1996)

[75] Ron, D., Shamir, A.: Quantitative analysis of the full bitcoin transaction graph

[76] Rosenfeld, M.: Analysis of bitcoin pooled mining reward systems. arXiv preprint arXiv:1112.4980 (2011)

[77] Rosenfeld, M.: Overview of colored coins. Technical report (2012)

[78] Rosenfeld, M.: Analysis of hashrate-based double spending. arXiv preprint arXiv:1402.2009 (2014)

[79] Schwartz, D., Youngs, N., Britto, A.: The ripple protocol consensus algorithm (2014)

[80] Sompolinsky, Y., Zohar, A.: Accelerating bitcoin's transaction processing

[81] Standards for Efficient Cryptography (SEC): SEC 2: Rec-
ommended elliptic curve domain parameters. Technical
report, Certicom Research (2000)

[82] STMicroelectronics: STM32F205xx STM32F207xx
datasheet, Doc ID 15818 Rev 9 (2012) [Online, Retrieved
March, 2014].

[83] Todd, P.: BIP 0065: OP_CHECKLOCKTIMEVERIFY.
`https://github.com/bitcoin/bips` (2014) [Online; accessed March 30th, 2014].

[84] Trusted Computing Group: TCG Specification Architecture Overview. (August 2007) Rev. 1.4.

[85] Univision Technology Inc.: UG-2864HSWEG01 datasheet,
SAS1-9046-B (2009) [Online, Retrieved March, 2014].

[86] Willett, J., Hidskes, M., Johnston, D., Gross, R., Schnei-
der, M.: The master protocol / mastercoin complete specification. `https://github.com/mastercoin-MSC/spec`
(2012)

[87] Wuille, P.: BIP 0062: Dealing with Malleability.
`https://github.com/bitcoin/bips` (2014) [Online; accessed March 10th, 2014].